MICHAEL D DIGATONO
333 TOIMI RD
BRIMSON MN 55602-8133

SMEAR TACTICS

SMEAR TACTICS

The Liberal Campaign to Defame America

BRAD MINER

HARPER

An Imprint of HarperCollins*Publishers*
www.harpercollins.com

HarperCollins books may be purchased for educational, business, or sales promotional use. For information, please write: Special Markets Department, HarperCollins Publishers, 10 East 53rd Street, New York, NY 10022.

FIRST EDITION

Library of Congress Cataloging-in-Publication Data

Miner, Brad.
    Smear tactics : the liberal campaign to defame America / Brad Miner. —1st ed.
        p.   cm.
    Includes bibliographical references and index.
    ISBN: 978-0-06-114014-3
    ISBN-10: 0-06-114014-7
    1. United States—Politics and government—2001–.   2. Liberalism—United States.   3. Conservatism—United States.   I. Title.
    JK275.M56   2007
    320.51'30973—dc22   2007034418

07   08   09   10   11   DIX/RRD   10   9   8   7   6   5   4   3   2   1

For Don Russell and Tom Smith, Buckeyes

CONTENTS

The mystic chords of memory, stretching from every battlefield and patriot grave to every living heart and hearthstone all over this broad land, will yet swell the chorus of the Union, when again touched, as surely they will be, by the better angels of our nature.

—ABRAHAM LINCOLN,
First Inaugural Address,
MARCH 4, 1861

I

VIPERS LOOSED

An Introduction to Smear Tactics

The serpent you cherished and warmed, bit the hand that nourished him, and gave you sufficient specimens of his talents, his gratitude, his justice, and his truth. When such vipers are let loose upon society, all distinction between virtue and vice are leveled, all respect for character is lost.

> —Abigail Adams in 1804 to Thomas Jefferson about James T. Callender, whom Jefferson had paid to smear her husband, John—and who then smeared Jefferson too.[1]

THE PRESIDENT OF THE UNITED STATES is a racist.

So say liberals, who also assert—vehemently—that George W. Bush is stupid, lazy, bloodthirsty, demagogic, venal, and, well, pick your most scarifying adjective. One Web site even declares the President to be the Antichrist. (Did you know that if you add up the numerical positions of the letters in his name as spelled in Hebrew the total is . . . 666? So claims www.bushisantichrist.com, although it is not explained why his middle name is not included or why Bush 43's name works, Bush 41's does not.

You can call Mr. Bush or any American a lot of things—insult him with bitterness and without restraint—but if you're really out to hurt him, call him racist, because then he'll be true and royally smeared. And if in addition to racist you can throw in fascist, well then, you've made the Perfect Smear. You've made the man an enemy of the state, not chief of state.

But whatever other faults W may have, racism—to take the first instance (we'll get to "fascist" soon enough)—certainly isn't among them. This is clear from, yes, his "compassionate conservatism" (tired as that phrase may be after nearly two terms of his presidency), which has led, among other things, from his commitment to spend upward of $15 billion to address the AIDS pandemic in Africa—a dramatic increase by any measure over all previous American administrations—and to his appointment of African Americans (and other minorities) to key cabinet positions. No other president of the United States has had a black secretary of state; Mr. Bush has had two. But, as the saying goes, *no good deed will go unpunished.* And the punishment was meted out with vigorous viciousness in the wake of the great storms that rocked the world a few years ago.

The year 2005 was indeed a low point for high water. At the start of the year, the whole world was still reeling from the emotional aftershocks of the Indian Ocean earthquake/tsunami that killed nearly 300,000 people, and it was not long after that America's National Oceanic and Atmospheric Administration (NOAA) was predicting a "95% to 100% chance of an above-normal hurricane season" in the Atlantic.

To paraphrase the poet: *They builded better than they knew.*

In the end, the Atlantic hurricanes of 2005 would obliterate all previous records. As NOAA reports, it was the first year ever with twenty-six named storms, the first with thirteen hurricanes, the first with three Category 5 storms, and the first in which four major hurricanes made landfall in the United States.

According to the American Red Cross, 2005 "was the 'worst-case scenario' for the United States," and it cites three of the storms as most destructive: Katrina, Rita, and Wilma.[2]

True enough, but were you aware that this period of increased hurricane activity actually began a decade earlier?[3] In fact, *all hurricane seasons since 1995 have been above normal.* However, in the wake of Katrina, this didn't stop some commentators, as you'll recall (we were all watching), from laying blame for the failure of New Orleans's levees squarely at the feet of President Bush. Such assertions were clearly the stuff of political smear tactics, however much of the sarcastic rants may have been selectively couched in the semblance of science.

You want sarcasm? The Web site SourceWatch, a sort of media encyclopedia for the American Left, begins its coverage of "George W. Bush: Hurricane Katrina" with this: "President George W. Bush was nearing the end of a month-long vacation at his Crawford, Texas, ranch on August 29, 2005, when Hurricane Katrina struck the Gulf Coast of the United States."[4] This pointed juxtaposition is certainly a subtle smear: What, we may ask, does the president's vacation have to do with the storm? What difference to the path of a natural disaster would the president's presence in the Oval Office have made? What difference, indeed, if he had been on the ground along the banks of Lake Pontchartrain piling up sandbags? The concurrence can only have been made by SourceWatch to evoke the popular liberal charge that Mr. Bush is lazy and uncaring. In an open letter to Mr. Bush, filmmaker Michael Moore mockingly wrote: "I know you didn't want to interrupt your vacation and I know how you don't like to get bad news. Plus you had fund-raisers to go to and mothers of dead soldiers to ignore and smear."[5] And as another liberal columnist put it: "George W. Bush, the least hardworking president in history, continued playing at his Texas ranch while his fellow citizens drowned and starved in New Orleans."[6] That's beginning to get a lot less subtle.

Others, of course, weren't subtle at all in leveling similar smears. There were some who accused the president of inaction and indifference before and after the storm, and a few who actually accused him of being a cause of the various calamities associated with Katrina—*even of the hurricane itself!*

But, to begin with, there were those charges of racism.

Now racism is a very serious matter, and the history of the United States since at least the 1960s has made the charge against an individual positively—and properly—toxic. It is a terrible smear when applied unjustly, and likely to wreck a political career if it can be made to stick—which is, after all, the point of a smear.

It is probably true that black citizens in New Orleans were affected by Katrina more than others were, but this was because they are disproportionately poor and live in the areas of the city most directly affected by the storm. Black poverty in the Big Easy has been in existence since the founding of America, and certainly has been the case under every president in the last century, Republican and Democrat. (More about this in a moment.) But that fact didn't stop CNN's Wolf Blitzer from reacting to scenes of the flooded city in such a way as to suggest something more sinister: "You simply get chills every time you see these poor individuals . . . as [commentator] Jack Cafferty just pointed out, so tragically, so many of these people, almost all of them that we see, are so poor and they are so black, and this is going to raise lots of questions for people who are watching this story unfold."[7]

I'm uncertain what it means to be "so black," but perhaps Blitzer was caught up in the emotions of the moment. Still, his observation that what his audience was witnessing would "raise lots of questions" was a portent of less temperate smears to come. He and Cafferty were apparently implying that in New Orleans, a city that prior to the storm was nearly 70 percent black, America was witnessing a kind of apartheid.* Perhaps Blitzer had read the *New York Times* article by David Gonzalez that said essentially the same thing through quotes from a number of well-known black leaders, but which also included this observation from a Brooklyn street vendor: "Blacks ain't worth it," he said (presumably with irony). "New Orleans is a hopeless case." This was a statement Gonzalez termed a "damning conclusion,"[8] though it is unclear if the street vendor's opinion was based upon historical or sociological research.

One may wonder in a similar way about the Rev. Jesse Jackson, who said "cities [such as New Orleans] had been dismissed by the Bush administration because Mr. Bush received few urban votes."[9]

"Our Bull Connor"

On the liberal Air America radio network, host Randi Rhodes claimed, in the spirit of Rev. Jackson and that street vendor, that Mr. Bush is indeed hopeless; that "deep down" the president actually felt joy about the loss of life in New Orleans. "If he thinks they vote Democrat," Rhodes told her listeners, "or if he thinks they're poor, or if he thinks they're in a blue state," he will refuse to rescue them.[10] And (in his imitable way) actor Colin Farrell told London's *Mirror* that if it had been white people who were

---

*This is exactly what the liberal Rense.com Web site did say: "New Orleans provides a grim reminder that 'Apartheid, American Style' is thriving in this nation."

suffering most in the storm's aftermath, "I don't have any f***ing doubt there would have been every single helicopter, plane and means that the government has trying to help."[11]

Liberals began expressing such sentiments within hours after the storm struck. Few seemed willing to acknowledge that, in America, responsibility for first response to natural disasters belongs to the localities and secondarily to the states. The role of the national government is tertiary, which is why when hurricanes, tornadoes, earthquakes, and fires strike we hear presidential declarations that affected localities are "disaster areas" only *after the fact*. At the liberal CommonDreams.org Web site, Sacha Boegem wrote that "Americans understand that when disaster strikes at home, the buck stops at the president's desk."[12] This may be literally true, but only because the president is the last resort: mayors and governors must request federal assistance, because the national government in Washington has no conventional authority to act as first responder. But these facts were irrelevant to those who took the opportunity provided by Katrina to smear the commander in chief as an indolent bigot.

During a celebrity appeal for hurricane victims televised by NBC, rapper Kanye West, whom *Time* magazine had called the "smartest man in pop music," famously proclaimed that "George Bush doesn't care about black people." But West was simply echoing the remarks of others, such as the aforementioned Farrell and *CBS Sunday Morning* commentator Nancy Giles, who asserted that "if the majority of the hardest hit victims of Hurricane Katrina in New Orleans were white people, they would not have gone for days without food and water."[13]

Most outrageous, Rep. Charles Rangel (D-NY) called the president "our Bull Connor," referring to the segregationist police commissioner from 1960s Birmingham, Alabama. Another New

Yorker, the Rev. Al Sharpton, evoked the same imagery, saying that Mr. Bush had taken blacks "from fire hoses to levees."

The frequency with which these spurious charges were repeated led commentator Ben Stein, writing at *The American Spectator*'s Web site, to suggest that Josef Goebbels would have appreciated the tactic: "Goebbels, for those of you too young to know, was Hitler's propaganda minister. He is credited with creating the concept of The Big Lie. The idea was that if you tell a lie big enough often enough, people will believe it."[14]

Stein goes on to reason that the impact of the big storms of 2005 upon African Americans was the result of geography, weather, poverty, and confusion. Not one of these conditions was created by George W. Bush.

In fact, as Deroy Murdock points out, federal anti-poverty spending, which directly benefits the African Americans affected by Katrina, rose more than 70 percent under President Bush.[15] During the Clinton administration, the poverty rate in the Big Easy was nearly 28 percent, but under President Bush the rate had dropped to just over 23 percent. Reacting to the smears of racism hurled at the president, Murdock, who is black, accuses Rangel, Sharpton, "and other friction-mongers" of plunging knives into "old racial wounds" and of exhuming the specter of bigotry in order to "inflame Americans who hardly need their generosity diluted with venom."*

---

*Al Sharpton was also a participant in one of the most notorious smears of the last several decades: the Tawana Brawley affair in which Brawley claimed she had been raped by six white men, though no evidence of sexual assault was found by physicians. Rev. Sharpton became Ms. Brawley's spokesman and named local prosecutor as not only the leader of a cover-up in the case but also as a racist and one of the alleged rapists. It was all a hoax, though Sharpton still claims that even if Tawana lied, she told a larger truth about black women and white men. Similar justifications were given years later in the Duke rape-case hoax to justify the smears against some of the school's lacrosse players.

At one point during Katrina coverage, former CBS news anchor Dan Rather told an interviewer that reporters covering the hurricane had "sucked up their guts and talked truth to power." To which journalist Mark Steyn remarked:

> Er, no. The facts they put in front of us were wrong, and they didn't talk truth to power. They talked to goofs in power, like New Orleans' Mayor Nagin and Police Chief [Edwin] Compass, and uncritically fell for every nutso yarn they were peddled. The media swallowed more bilge than if they'd been lying down with their mouths open as the levee collapsed. Ten thousand dead! Widespread rape and murder! A 7-year-old gang-raped and then throat-slashed! It was great stuff—and none of it happened. No gang-raped 7-year-olds. None.[16]

And why did the media swallow the "bilge," as Steyn puts it? As both Steyn and Stein agree, because it was a "media riot." And that riot continued into the next year.

In February 2006 (nearly six months after the storm), the Associated Press received video and audio tapes of pre-Katrina-landfall conversations among government officials at all levels, and there was a frenzy of accusation that Mr. Bush "had been warned!" But as blogger Bob (Confederate Yankee) Owens put it:

> In its substance, the video reveals nothing that was not already known from previously released transcripts and government investigations. But in politics, images carry a power far beyond written words, and the video, played again and

again on cable television, instantly provided new fuel for an emotional debate.

This debate is not a story of substance, but one of emotion.[17]

And Owens points out that response to Hurricane Katrina was "by far the largest, fastest rescue in American history," though he also acknowledges that many mistakes were made by most of the governments involved, beginning with the poor construction of the levees, and including inadequate evacuation plans.

"Leadership collapsed," Owens writes, "and in some cases, hindered the rescue effort. There is plenty of blame to go around, and no shortage of imaginative ideas to help boost our response capabilities for future storms to levels never before imagined."

Indeed. Yet when *Popular Mechanics* magazine conducted four months of post-Katrina interviews in an attempt to understand exactly what happened, it concluded that a number of myths had been popularized in the press.[18] The magazine doesn't say it, but I will: the liberal press.

> MYTH: Government was slow to respond.
> REALITY: Response was "by far the largest—and fastest—rescue effort in U.S. history. . . ."
>
> MYTH: Katrina was a once-in-a-lifetime super storm.
> REALITY: Katrina was actually a Category 3 hurricane when it hit New Orleans, and the damage was mostly the result of the radius of the storm and its powerful storm surge—a result of its path over the Gulf of Mexico's shallow northern shelf.

Bear with me on this; it's important.

MYTH: The levees failed because of malfeasance in their very
        construction.
REALITY: When the Army Corps of Engineers pulled up sections of the
        levee for examination, they were found to have been
        constructed exactly to specifications.

MYTH: New Orleans descended into chaos and even anarchy.
REALITY: As we've seen, this simply wasn't true. As *Popular
        Mechanics* summarizes, "truth was the first casualty of the
        information breakdown that followed the storm."

MYTH: Evacuation plans were inadequate.
REALITY: 1.2 million people fled New Orleans—out of a population of
        1.5 million—and they did it in thirty-eight hours instead of
        the planned seventy-two.

These facts are essential in understanding that the charges leveled against President Bush were indeed a media riot—a liberal smear campaign against the president they love to hate.

And, by the way, on the subject of those levees: The project to build them up was authorized in 1965, which is to say that presidents Johnson, Nixon, Ford, Carter, Reagan, Bush, Clinton, and Bush all had the opportunity to lavish money on the ongoing efforts to make them capable of withstanding hurricanes—and, indeed, all did. In fact, the administration of George W. Bush actually spent more money over the five years prior to Katrina on "key New Orleans flood-control projects" than the Clinton administration did in its last five years.[19] And never forget that the Crescent City sits in a bowl—actually below sea level (and below the level of the Mississippi River that runs through it). According to the *Washington Post,* Lt. Gen. Carl Strock, chief of the Army Corps of Engineers, said: ". . . '[M]ore money would not have prevented the drowning of the city, since . . . the levees that failed were already completed projects'. Strock has also said that the marsh-restoration project would not have done much to diminish Katrina's storm surge, which passed east of the coastal wetlands."[20]

Is this clear enough? No action by anyone before, during, or after the storm could have saved New Orleans. No one is to blame for what happened, and what happened was actually a remarkable testament to the resilience and charity of the American people. But what use is a hurricane to the Left if they can't blame it on President Bush?

Hurricane Bush

When Michael Moore accused Mr. Bush of lolling about his ranch in Crawford, Texas, in the aftermath of Katrina and of ignoring and smearing the mothers of dead soldiers, he was making reference to antiwar activist Cindy Sheehan, with whom Mr. Bush had once met (as he regularly meets with the families of the men and women killed in battle), but with whom he refused to meet again after she had raised the temper of her rhetoric about the war in Iraq. Sheehan herself had insisted, the day before Moore wrote his letter to the president, that the hurricane itself was Mr. Bush's fault—its devastation a result of his "environmental policies and his killing policies."[21]

Both Robert F. Kennedy Jr., writing at the Huffington Post blog, and Ross Gelbspan, writing in the *Boston Globe,* suggested the same thing: that Mr. Bush (his associates or his policies) actually caused the *intensity* of Hurricane Katrina. Kennedy asserted that the Bush administration's refusal to aggressively reduce CO_2 emissions contributed to global warming. "Our destructive addiction [to fossil fuels] has given us a catastrophic war in the Middle East and—now—Katrina is giving our nation a glimpse of the climate chaos we are bequeathing our children."[22] Gelbspan wrote that the hurricane may have been "nicknamed Katrina by the National Weather Service. Its real name is global warming."[23] And he directly linked an uptick in global warming to "big oil and big coal," industries that scored their biggest political victories yet when George W. Bush was elected and reelected president—and subsequently took suggestions from the industry for his climate and energy policies.

Kennedy specifically blamed Gov. Haley Barbour of Mississippi, a Republican, who in 2001 had lobbied the Bush administration to oppose carbon dioxide restrictions. "Now," Kennedy wrote with solemnity, "we are all learning what it's like to reap the whirlwind of fossil fuel dependence . . ."

And the liberal advocacy group MoveOn.org flatly stated that global warming "almost certainly increased the force of Hurricane Katrina."[24]

These are astonishing assertions about the sinister intent and effect of a president who, at that point, had been in power for barely five years.

Two matters are immediately at issue here. The first is the NOAA data on the period during which increased hurricane activity has been observed: for a decade, the first half of which came during the presidency of Bill Clinton. The second matter is the allegation, frequently made by scientists associated with the United Nations, that global warming was the cause of (or caused the intensity of) Katrina and other recent hurricanes. This is not the place for a lengthy digression about CO_2 levels, greenhouse gases, and other technical facts and fallacies pertaining to the earth's mean temperature and its effect on the weather, but it is worth mentioning that, just about a year before Katrina hit, three distinguished scientists were able to assert with confidence that global warming is largely a myth. If worldwide temperatures are really on the rise, they wrote, neither "satellite nor . . . balloon records [used to catalog temperature data] can find it." Indeed, we now have "a quarter-century of . . . balloon and satellite data, both screaming that the U.N.'s climate models have failed. . . ." And this is only part of the evidence against the theory.[25] Another climatologist wrote in response to the global-warming-causes-hurricanes meme:

> Claims that Katrina is due to global warming are not supported by scientific or historical evidence, but that doesn't stop the hysteria. Beliefs that hurricanes have increased in frequency and severity are simply false. The only measurable increase is in the cost of repairing the damage. This is mostly explained by natural cost increases, exploitation of demand for materials and more people living in regions of climate hazards.[26]

Are they right, and the many other scientists wrong who say that global warming is a fact? And if temperatures are rising, is it because of human activity or because of naturally occurring weather cycles? These are good questions, but not entirely on point here. It's often asserted that the consensus among scientists is that the earth's mean temperature *is* rising, but as the novelist Michael Crichton has put it: "There is no such thing as consensus science. If it's consensus, it isn't science. If it's science, it isn't consensus. Period."* Some proof of this is found in a recent post at the blog site of *Scientific American* magazine, which made much of the fact that opinion researchers at Yale University found that 83 percent of respondents to a February 2007 survey called global warming a "serious" problem.[27] But as James Taranto of the *Wall Street Journal* wryly notes, that very same survey found that 58 percent agreed with the statement that "as the Bible says, the world was literally created in six days," and Taranto concludes: "So according to *Scientific American*, the biblical story of creation has only slightly less scientific merit than global warming."[28] Consensus is everywhere! At the Web site of the prestigious Woods Hole Oceanographic Institute, you can read a scientific paper on how "slow changes to our climate . . . will affect humans and the habitability of our planet." Maybe, the authors suggest, our usual thinking about global warming is flawed: "It ignores the well-established fact that Earth's climate has changed rapidly in the past and could change rapidly in the future. The issue centers on the paradox that global warming could instigate a new Little Ice Age in the northern hemisphere."[29]

Thomas Sowell has observed that given the contradictory arguments "you might not be willing to go along with those who are prepared to ruin the economy, sacrificing jobs and the na-

---

*Among the best summaries of the various dilemmas was written by Dr. Henry I. Miller, a physician and molecular biologist, in the *San Francisco Chronicle*: "If we are to meet economic, environmental and public health challenges, we need plenty of options and opportunities for innovation—and the wealth to pursue them. In society, as in biology, survival demands adaptation. But in large and small ways, unimaginative, short-sighted politicians and venal activists have conspired to limit our options, constrain economic growth and make real solutions elusive."

tional standard of living on the altar to the latest in an unending series of crusades, conducted by politicians and other people seeking to tell everyone else how to live."[30] But the point to be made here is that the scientific *facts* are not settled—except, that is, for one: *Despite liberal assertions to the contrary, it is impossible that in the course of five years the decisions and policies of the president of the United States, his political party, and his administration created atmospheric or oceanographic conditions sufficient to affect the world's weather.*

Anyway, we know for certain that such changes were well under way years before Republicans took control of Washington, D.C.

Of course, as we'll shortly see when we consider the history of political smears, this sort of calumny comes inevitably to the occupant of the Oval Office. It is also true that in the wake of Katrina and Rita, the Bush administration doubtless deserved criticism for its responses to the disasters—as did other agencies: federal, state, and local. However, the temper of the comments of Sheehan, Kennedy, and Gelbspan are the stuff of smear: each in his or her own way has gone beyond the truth in an attempt to demean a public figure, in this case the commander in chief.

In this they are abetted by mass media, which long ago learned that villainy makes great copy. Thus, in the aftermath of Katrina, newspapers, television, and radio were reporting as fact the following misstatements:[31]

- the New Orleans Superdome was the site of rampant post-hurricane murder and rapine (New Orleans mayor Ray Nagin on *Oprah*)
- rescuers were frequently fired upon by angry Gulf Coast residents (CNN)

- "40,000 Could Be Lost in Hurricane" (*Editor & Publisher*)
- many patients in hospitals and nursing homes died awaiting evacuation (CNN)

And although a retraction was later published, the true low-water mark of objectivity and taste came when Randall Robinson, self-proclaimed "social justice advocate," wrote that "black hurricane victims in New Orleans have begun eating corpses to survive. Four days after the storm, thousands of blacks in New Orleans are dying like dogs."[32] One is not sure if the specter, once again, of Mr. Bush's alleged racism is as sickening as the implication of Robinson, who is black, that African Americans in New Orleans were acting out some kind of real-life zombie movie.

This sort of heated rhetoric, always inflamed primarily by animosity toward Mr. Bush and secondarily toward the Federal Emergency Management Agency, had short-term consequences. As journalist Michael Fumento writes: "As to the military . . . the only heroes to come out of the debacle, the fast-flying rumors forced them to launch combat operations before switching to rescue mode. They also had to wear heavy body armor in terrific heat, which I know from experience slows you down in those conditions. . . . [T]he last thing stranded residents needed was hampered rescuers."[33] In fact, the final death toll from Hurricane Katrina (throughout Louisiana—not just in New Orleans) was 1,077.[34] Six people died at the Superdome: four from natural causes, one from a drug overdose, and one was a suicide.

A very large number of left-wingers insisted that Mr. Bush should have seen it coming, but hindsight is always 20/20. Still . . . it's more than a little disconcerting to read at the most popular liberal blog of them all, Daily Kos, that: "I feel it necessary to demand that we right now begin criticizing this president for his policy decisions, which have exacerbated the tragedy, his dereliction of duty as president, his overall callousness and his inert response."[35] This was written on August 31, 2005—the day the storm dissipated.

Certainly George W. Bush is not responsible for the hurricanes and largely not responsible for the problems related to the disaster's aftermath, and the criticisms of him in this regard often descended into smear tactics. This is nothing new for Mr. Bush, who seems to attract this sort of thing as few presidents ever have. As a rule presidents of the United States have often been the target of libel, slander, insult, and smear. Indeed, there are probably no exceptions to the rule.

Still, George W. Bush, whatever his merits and his faults, has probably been the most smeared president in history. As liberal commentator Mort Kondracke wrote in the months leading up to the 2004 Election, "the muddy epithets thrown at President Bush outweigh those thrown at Democrats by tons."[36]

We'll return shortly to the specific attacks (especially the allegations of fascism) made on Mr. Bush, but first let us consider the more general meaning and history of smear tactics.

Defining the Smear

What exactly is a smear?

It is a falsehood designed to discredit a public figure. The word derives from the same root as the other sense of the word—its verb form, meaning to rub on, as one would an oil or ointment. Indeed, the etymology begins with an ancient German word, *smero*, which means ointment, and that certainly evokes the play-ground bully whose taunting "rubs it in."

The public-figure part is important in the definition. It's not that one private citizen can't smear another private citizen; it's just that when that happens we call it slander or libel (about which more shortly) or bad manners, but the world "smear" is best re-served to refer to attacks on men and women in the public eye.

Smears often come in bunches, which is why the words "smear" and "campaign" are often linked. Because smears, smear cam-paigns, and the tactics involved therein almost inevitably involve lies or distortions, the smears themselves are either slanderous or libelous. To refresh the distinction: think library for libel. A *libel is a lie about a person told in a book*. Well, in print, anyway—it could be in a book, a newspaper, a magazine, or a blog. A slander, on the other hand, is an oral lie, which is to say it's made in speaking: on radio or television, in a speech or even in a casual conversation. Libel is a whole lot easier to prove in court, since the evidence is right there on a page in black and white, and since a slanderous statement usually requires a judge or jury to take one person's word over another's.

But, whether libel or slander, in the United States of America such statements can generally be employed with impunity against public figures. In a famous case before the Supreme Court, *New York Times v. Sullivan* (1964), a standard known as "actual malice" was established. This means that simple misstatements about a public figure are not in themselves sufficient grounds for a convic-tion under the laws of slander and libel. There must also be a provable intent to defame the person in question; what the courts call a "reckless disregard" for the truth.

That may seem cut-and-dried, but many plaintiffs have learned that suing the person or medium who has defamed them is pretty much a thankless task. Lawsuits tend to keep the lies alive and even spread them more widely, and "actual malice" can be difficult to establish since it requires "smoking gun" proof of some kind, which the printed words themselves in a libel case rarely do.

The dictionary—the *Shorter Oxford* in this case—defines a smear as "a slanderous story . . . circulated to discredit a public figure," but it can also be a *libelous* statement. It's all the same to the person whose good name is being trashed. These days we seem not to appreciate the notion of a spotless reputation, but it was once thought to be essential—so important, in fact, that men would fight duels over certain insults.

If we imagine this somewhat antiquated idea of a "good name" or of a "faultless character" as literally a clean, white garment, we can understand the origin of the term "mudslinging." When a man's honor was soiled by slander, he reacted with anger and revulsion. Yet an insult, per se, is not and never was necessarily a smear, and the duelist who took the "most grievous possible exception" to another man's remark was often spoiling for a fight.

An example:

Before he became president, Andrew Jackson fought a duel with Charles Dickinson, who had libeled the future commander in chief as a coward (actually, a scoundrel, a poltroon, *and* a coward, which is redundant) over a horse-racing bet, and had also slandered Jackson's wife, Rachel. Jackson called out the blackguard. They met at dawn, stood the approved twenty-four paces apart, and exchanged shots. Both were hit, but Dickinson was killed—as Jackson fired, he swooned and fell. Jackson suffered greatly from the wound he received, and yet he was lucky: Dickinson was considered the best shot in all of Tennessee and was believed to have killed more than two dozen men in other duels. All this over words.

Shakespeare's Romeo was a duelist, albeit a reluctant one. But before he fatally crossed swords with Tybalt, he responded to an insult—from a friend in fact—by joking to himself, "He jests at scars that never felt a wound," which is the better way to respond: no blood gets spilled when a man shrugs off a slur. Insults may be cutting and infuriating, but they may also be signs of intimate friendship: Teenage boys especially, such as Romeo and his pal Mercutio, revel in calling one another the kind of names that if spoken by a stranger would be fighting words. But no matter how shocking, no matter how hard somebody jumps on you (the etymology of the word *insult*), the effect of the affront is not the same as a smear. Insults may be answered either in the manner of Romeo or of Andrew Jackson, but in either case the offense is expiated. But smears—if they are effective—may stick to a reputation for a lifetime, as did the lead from Dickinson's bullet, which stayed lodged in Jackson's ribs, causing Old Hickory pain for the rest of his life.

Back then, a tarnished reputation might be settled in a duel. These days, it's more likely to be settled in court—often, however, with limited success.

A Distinction

The difference between an insult and a smear is important. Insults are nasty comments made about a person that properly should be shrugged off according to the children's rule: "Sticks and stones may break my bones, but words will never hurt me." This may be hard to do, of course. Jackson couldn't do it.

When former president Teddy Roosevelt called Woodrow Wilson a "Byzantine logothete" (in other words, a mere *functionary*), President Wilson can't have been pleased, though he probably shrugged it off. Presidents have to take this sort of thing. William Duane wrote to inform George Washington that he was "treacherous in private friendship . . . and a hypocrite in public life, the world will be puzzled to decide whether you are an apostate or an imposter, whenever you have abandoned good principles, or whether you ever had any. . . ."[37]

The Father of Our Country probably couldn't have cared less, although—again—men of his generation did not take lightly aspersions cast upon their good names. But it's when insults become enshrined in legal proceedings and in ongoing media campaigns that unkind words cut deepest.

When former Reagan administration labor secretary Raymond Donovan was acquitted of corruption charges in 1987, he asked a rhetorical question of the reporters who had been covering his trial (and exploiting it to hurt the Reagan administration): "Where do I go to get my reputation back?" Donovan understood what President Bush faces: no matter what happens to him throughout the rest of his life, there will always be people who will believe Mr. Bush to be a lazy, moronic liar, thanks to the depth and breadth of the smears consistently leveled against him over the last decade.

The attacks on President Bush are the state of smear artistry in the present day, and we hear often—and from different points along the political spectrum—that the level of incivility in American politics is lower even than those New Orleans levees: first Clinton, now Bush, and we all seem to be faceup with our mouths open as the brackish water rushes in. Is this true? Are the smears of the Right as bad as those of the Left? Are the smears of the 2000s worse than the 1800s?

Not by a long shot. So let's see how bad things used to be, and how smear tactics first became the American way of politicking.

A Short History of the Smear

We can't know for certain when the first smear campaign sullied America's cultural or political life. All smears are verbal, but—as noted above—some may be oral, and if a 17th- or 18th-century whispering campaign (a slander) was not also written down—in newspapers, diaries, whatever (becoming thus a libel)—it is lost to us now.

But one of the first of which we do have a record played out in the summer of 1721.

James Franklin was a famous printer, although his celebrity has been eclipsed by that of his apprentice and younger brother, Benjamin, who began working at his brother's Boston print shop when he was just twelve. (He would flee to Philadelphia to begin in earnest his own career five years later.) Out of this shop James published the *New England Courant*, which launched in August of '21 and didn't take long to make an impression on the city, once the elder Franklin decided to take on Boston's most notable citizen, the Congregationalist minister and author Cotton Mather, which he did in a series of articles attacking the Puritan clergyman's very progressive endorsement of inoculations for smallpox.

Inoculation against the disease was controversial, because it seemed in the popular mind to defy common sense: How could exposure to an infectious disease actually prevent the disease? It did, though the state-of-the-art was lacking—Edward Jenner, the real inventor of vaccination, did not settle the matter for another seventy-five years. But *variolation* (an ancient Chinese technique of removing pus from the sores of an infected person and inoculating healthy people with it) had been introduced to Britain some months before Franklin and Mather locked horns, and, although it remained a divisive issue for many, for a man of a scientific inclination such as Mather it made perfect sense.

Ben Franklin, another man of science, came to endorse the practice—and to admire Mather (*Bonifacius: An Essay Upon the Good* by Mather was one of the books Ben would say gave him "a Turn of Thinking that had an Influence on some of the principal future Events of my Life"[38])—but his brother was adamantly opposed. (Ben's conversion to variolation came too late to save his own son, who died of the pox at age four.) According to Eric Burns,[39] James let loose one of his reporters, John Checkley, whose stories "frightened many a reader. It made them scornful of inoculation and skeptical of the Mathers [Cotton and his father, Increase]. In fact, as far as some people were concerned, it cast doubt on all figures of authority. . . ." A smallpox epidemic was even then sweeping through Boston, and to James Franklin it seemed certain that Mather was aiding its spread, and he said so. (Perhaps there was some cold recompense made here by destiny—through the agency of James Franklin—to the "man of science" for Mather's earlier defense of the Salem Witch Trials.) The *Courant* railed, and Mather, who had for so long seemed above reproach, suddenly found not only that his probity and honor were under attack but that he was made a laughingstock, and this is when it really got ugly.

Mather fought back. His nephew, Thomas Walter, wrote in one of the *Courant*'s competitors, the *News-Ledger*, that Franklin's was . . .

. . . a "Notorious, Scandalous Paper . . . fullfreighted with Nonsense, Unmannerliness, Railery, Prophaneness, Immorality, Arrogancy, Calumnies, Lyes." This was polemic in the accepted eighteenth-century manner. But when the letter writer stooped to accuse the Boston physicians [whom the *Courant* had organized against inoculation] of having banded together and clandestinely formed a "Hell-Fire Club . . . like to that . . . scandalous Club . . . set up in London to insult the most sacred Principles of the Christian Religion," he went beyond invective acceptable even then.[40]

The whole affair, which continued on into 1722, became known as the War of the Pamphlets.

A characteristic of the smear campaign emerges here: unfair attacks are made upon people who very well may deserve comeuppance. The trouble is that smears lack objectivity, they go overboard from argument into mischaracterization—which, after all, is what makes them smears—and they ultimately do as much, if not more, harm to the "smear merchant" as to the object of the smear.

James Franklin was, indeed, a smear merchant, and was notorious as the leading practitioner of that dubious art until the more notorious reign of the greatest of the 18th-century's mudslingers, James Callender.

A Viper Loosed

In the epigraph at the beginning of this chapter, Abigail Adams laughs through gritted teeth at the way Callender repaid Thomas Jefferson's patronage. The Sage of Monticello had employed Cal-

lender in the presidential election of 1800 to sully the reputation
of his opponent, Abigail's husband, President John Adams. Callender would eventually bite the hand that fed him.

Callender, a Scotsman, had come to the attention of Jefferson's
Democratic-Republican Party as the journalist who had uncovered and publicized Alexander Hamilton's affair with Mrs.
Maria Reynolds. Hamilton, like Adams, was a leader of the
Federalist Party, and the attacks on Hamilton's reputation (he
admitted the affair but denied other more serious charges) make
for a long story—treated beautifully by William Safire in his
novel *Scandalmonger*—but the upshot is that the Hamilton-
Reynolds-Callender affair led to the Sedition Act of 1798, by
which the Federalists made it illegal to "write, print, utter, or
publish" attacks against public officials. In a fine historical irony,
one of the journalists arrested was the publisher of Philadelphia's *Aurora*, Benjamin Franklin Bache, grandnephew of James
Franklin.

The Act also provided the Jeffersonians with a powerful campaign issue.

But that was not enough for Jefferson. He let loose his "viper"
to slither after Adams, which Callender did in a series of articles,
paid for by Jefferson, which ran in the *Richmond Examiner* beginning in 1799.

Dredging up the pro-monarchy charges that always dogged
Adams, Callender accused the president of being "mentally
deranged," planning to crown himself king, and grooming
John Quincy as his heir to the throne. Adams was a "hideous
hermaphroditical character, which has neither the force of a
man, nor the gentleness and sensibility of a woman."[41]

Monarchist. Madman. Hermaphrodite. For good measure, he also called Adams a whoremonger.

Of course, Jefferson got much of the same from newspapers in Adams's neck of the woods, especially (no surprise) the *New England Courant*, which proclaimed that if he were elected:

> Murder, robbery, rape, adultery, and incest will be openly taught and practised, the air will be rent with the cries of distress, the soil soaked with blood, and the nation black with crimes. Where is the heart that can contemplate such a scene without shivering with horror?[42]

We know what Abigail Adams thought of Callender's attacks on her husband (which, by the way, led to Callender's arrest and imprisonment), but her point about Jefferson having been bit by the serpent referred to Callender's later articles "exposing" the third president's affair with a slave, Sally Hemings.

For his tireless work on behalf of the new president, Callender had expected to receive payback in the form of some kind of patronage appointment. But Jefferson knew the sort of man Callender was and spurned him. Hell hath no fury, apparently, like a scribbler scorned. In 1802, Callender published (in the same Richmond paper) the blockbusting claim that Jefferson "kept, as his concubine, one of his own slaves. . . . Her name is Sally." He also wrote that the president had "several children" with her.[43] According to Callender, this was the common knowledge of many people in Virginia, but it was potentially bad news to other Americans, except perhaps to some Federalists, who welcomed the revelations. Jefferson refused comment, but the scandal stayed with him for the rest of his administration and for the rest of his life.

Now we know that Callender's charges against John Adams were utterly false. But was the story of the Hemings-Jefferson union a smear or simply journalism, albeit nasty? Callender clearly intended to harm his former patron, which suggests that "actual malice" was present in the "exposure" of the alleged affair. But— and it's a big but—the surest defense against libel in court, whether a court of law or the court of public opinion, is the truth.

This may actually be a rare case in which the smear doesn't also involve a libel . . . but, if it is a smear, it's because of the intent: Callender definitely sought to defame Jefferson. He believed he knew what people thought about miscegenation (an ugly word from the dark recesses of our history), and he believed his articles would damage the Jefferson presidency. Callender probably believed the charges himself and, therefore, knew that if the president decided to take him to court Jefferson risked failing in his prosecution of the case precisely because what Callender alleged was true, as indeed it may have been. I write "may have been," as earlier I put *exposure* between scare quotes, because there is evidence in the matter of the union that is either exculpatory or incriminating depending upon one's interpretation. Modern cellular analysis proves that the descendants of Sally Hemings (she was the mother of seven and the grandmother and great-grandmother of scores) do indeed carry Jefferson-family DNA. What can't be established conclusively is from *which* Jefferson the genetic material came. It may indeed have come from Thomas; it may have come from his brother, Randolph; it may have come from one or another nephew . . . no one can say. What we can say is what Paul Rahe, a member of one of the commissions that has investigated the genetic links, has written: "[T]here is . . . one thing that we do know, and it is damning enough. Despite the distaste he expressed for the propensity of slaveholders and their relatives to abuse their power, Jefferson either engaged in such abuse himself or tolerated it on the part of one or more members of his extended family."[44]

But is that really inherent in the DNA results? Yes, because Jefferson was too great a scientist—albeit an amateur one—to disbelieve the evidence before his own eyes—the Hemings children bore striking resemblance to the Jeffersons.

Callender intensely disliked Jefferson and African Americans, and certainly was a broken, bitter man who shortly after his "Sally" articles were published got drunk, fell into the James River, and drowned. He'd misjudged the public reaction to the charges in Virginia and elsewhere, in part because the Sally *slander* had been around for some time (Hemings had been with Jefferson for fifteen years when Callender first published the story) before it became a *libel*, and in part because, dark secret though miscegenation was, it was an open secret.

A sad and peculiar postscript to this story involves Alexander Hamilton. During the election of 1800, he wrote a pamphlet attacking Adams, which helped elect Jefferson. Why this Federalist attacked another Federalist remains in dispute. What is not in dispute is that the election was decided in the House of Representatives—not between Adams and Jefferson, but between Jefferson and the man ostensibly chosen by the Democratic-Republicans as his running mate: Aaron Burr. So disliked was Jefferson by congressional Federalists that they initially supported Burr. But then Hamilton published another of his poison-pen attacks on Burr (more justified in this case), and, after thirty-six ballots, the voting broke Jefferson's way. Thus he became president and Burr, as the runner-up, vice president. But Burr, who was supposed to have ceded immediately to Jefferson and had not, alienated many in his party, most especially President Jefferson, and when the election of 1804 came around, Burr was summarily dropped from the ticket. When Burr heard that Hamilton had subsequently slandered him at a New York dinner party, he challenged the former treasury secretary to the Weehawken, New Jersey, duel that cost Hamilton his life.

There was certainly a time when smears were very costly indeed.

Why Smear?

We know that smear tactics have hovered over American politics practically from the start, but this fact does not tell us why. Human nature being what it is, we may conclude that since men lie frequently for advantage—lies about political opponents are to be expected. True enough, but there is often an important qualifier: smears flourish where there is an imbalance of power.

This means that those out of power are more inclined to smear those in power. Indeed, it may even be the case that the intensity of smears is directly proportional to a sense of powerlessness. In the contemporary political context, it should indicate that the "Left" is more likely to smear the "Right," since the former group's political authority is waning. And the facts do indicate this— despite the 2006 midterm elections results in which Democrats regained control of Congress.

But this is not to say that the so-called Right—conservatives and Republicans—do not engage in smear tactics. They do, because—despite many electoral successes—their hold on political power is tenuous, and their fear of seeing the scales tip left is sufficient to make smears alluring.

Although this is a generalization, "conservative" smears have tended to be different from "liberal" smears, in that the former do not intend to defame America. Attacks on individuals are ugly and reprehensible, but if conservatives pile on Cindy Sheehan, the intent is to discredit her and the appeal of her message in the media. Liberal media attacks on the abuses at the Abu Ghraib prison in Iraq, on the other hand, seem intent on libeling America's armed forces. Does it matter whether one smears an individual or an institution? Perhaps not in the short run. But for the future of the nation it matters very much.

To be blunt: the political landscape is littered with ruined reputations, and the nation is largely unharmed. It's a little bit of hell if you're the person on the business end of a smear, but, in fact, the rest of us go on, pretty much unaffected. But when the media pile on, as they did during the Vietnam War and more recently with stories from Iraq such as Abu Ghraib, the very institution of military service is smeared. To the extent that such stories undermine the armed forces—by diminishing recruitments or damaging public esteem for the profession or arms—America itself is threatened.

When best-selling authors accuse politically motivated Christians of advocating an American theocracy, faith itself is being smeared. When some industries and many executives are attacked, it's often entrepreneurship and free markets that are being smeared. When men such as J. Edgar Hoover or Joseph McCarthy are vilified, it is often patriotism that is being smeared. This is true even when, as in the cases of Hoover and McCarthy, there is much about those patriots that deserves criticism; when, in fact, the men themselves may have been utterly odious.

Time was when the dominant viewpoint in American media was anti-anticommunism. Defects in the American way of life were seen—usually sub rosa—as solvable through the gradual implementation of a "managed economy" and "directed politics." Thus the Soviet experiment was worthy of support, and those who opposed communism there—or its advocacy here—were seen by the liberal elites as enemies of progressive thought. Thus, anti-anticommunism. As Linda Chavez recently wrote:

> Instead of recognizing communism as a clear and present danger to freedom and liberty here and abroad, many liberals decided the real threat to those values came from anti-communism itself. Anti-anti-communism became the defining characteristic of American liberals, who have never fully recovered their credibility with the American people when it comes to protecting the nation.[45]

She goes on to point out that the inheritors of this tendency today often advocate what may be called "anti-anti-terrorism."

With communism all but utterly discredited by history, and given the toll terrorism has inflicted on people in America, it may seem incredible that anybody could take up the cause of, say, Islamofascism.

But that's not what is happening.

It isn't Islamofascism that the Left advocates; it is anti-Americanism, which is what was behind the anti-anticommunism in an earlier generation. Although as late as the 1980s there were many liberal intellectuals who believed in the promise of social-ism, there were not so many who believed that the Soviet Union was the seat and source of virtue in the world. What was attrac-tive about the USSR, however, was its value as a counterweight to American power, what was wrong with American power was its embrace of democracy, and what's wrong with democracy is the way it offers access to power to any American. The more democracy we have, the less power is vested in elites, and the more those elites hunker down for the power struggle.

As Michael Barone has written, the anti-Americanism of liberal elites is a fairly recent phenomenon in American history.

Most Harvard professors in the 1940s, 1950s, and early 1960s felt a responsibility to help the United States prevail against its totalitarian enemies. But in the later stages of the Vietnam War—a war begun by elite liberals—elites on campuses began taking an adversary posture toward their own country. Later, with globalization, a transnational mind-set grew among corporate and professional elites. Legal elites, too: Some Supreme Court justices have taken to citing foreign law as one basis for interpreting the U.S. Constitution. This gap between transnational elites and the patriotic public has reverberations in partisan politics.[46]

Call them elites or Mandarins or the Anointed, they are a class of postmodernist true believers who are convinced that their intelligence and their education and their philosophy have made them more capable than the rest of us to govern America. However, failing any substantial appeal to the electorate, they must maneuver for power by means of stealth.

This book's final chapter will consider how all of us living in a republican democracy can rediscover how to carry on political conversations—and to speak to one another on any contentious subject—without descending into a kind of intellectual cannibalism. For now, let's try to be clear about just who the flesh-eaters are.

They may be of either political party. They may be of no political party. Their reasons for engaging in what is often called "the politics of personal destruction" will vary from smear merchant to smear merchant: sometimes the attacks will be personal; sometimes they'll be motivated by ideology.* Up close, one slanderer may appear elegant, while another may seem disheveled. The smear itself may be a subtle, whispered insinuation; it may be a headline in tomorrow's tabloid. The patron . . . demon (certainly no patron saint) of smear tactics is Shakespeare's Iago, the scheming spreader of lies whose treachery leads a great man to commit a great sin: Othello murders his beloved Desdemona. The great irony of the play is the early speech of the plotter in which he says:

> *Good name in man and woman, dear my lord,*
> *Is the immediate jewel of their souls:*
> *Who steals my purse steals trash; 'tis something, nothing;*
> *'Twas mine, 'tis his, and has been slave to thousands:*
> *But he that filches from me my good name*
> *Robs me of that which not enriches him*
> *And makes me poor indeed.*

Iago knows only too well the way to destroy the great man, and it's a destruction that Iago believes he richly deserves to deliver.

---

*Writing in the *Indianapolis Star*, Ken Bode noted that when Conrad Hilton was asked what he'd like to say to the patrons of his hotels, he advised, " 'Please put the curtain inside the tub.' Commenting recently to a Des Moines audience about how to handle negative campaigns, Hillary Clinton was less droll. 'When you're attacked, you have to deck your opponent,' she advised. Straightforward, clear, knife-fight simple."

And this is a thing most practitioners of the smear have in common: They believe themselves justified, and the justification almost always amounts to one thing: arrogance. They believe they are better than you and I. They are an elite.

They are the Anointed. They are Mandarins. And they are *really* pissed off that the rest of us won't acknowledge their superior wisdom.

The economist Thomas Sowell, from whom I've borrowed the word "Anointed," makes a distinction between two visions governing political life: the constrained and the unconstrained. These visions are never pure, and they're often hard to figure out, but (and this is a short summary) the constrained is what we saw in the American Revolution, the unconstrained in the French Revolution. As Sowell puts it: "Robespierre sought a solution, Hamilton a trade-off."[47] The American revolutionaries took men as they are; the French tried to remake human nature. "Implicit in the unconstrained vision is a profound inequality between the conclusions of 'persons of narrow views' and those with 'cultivated minds.' "[48]

In Hamlet's weak moments, this is the way he saw the world: " 'tis an unweeded garden,/That grows to seed; things rank and gross in nature/Possess it. . . ." The unconstrained elitists cannot abide an untidy world, especially one in which their enlightened views are not dominant. They want a thousand flowers to bloom.

On the other hand, the more temperate man has humility sufficient to recognize that he is not, himself, the wellspring of rectitude. As Federalist #51 puts it (in language generally ascribed to James Madison): "If men were angels, no government would be necessary." But we're not angels, and so we must be constrained (be *democrats*—small "d")—the main constraint being the humanity of others, with all Man's foibles and follies. *That's* equality.

What does this have to do with smears? Why is the elitist more likely to resort to smear tactics? Again, Prof. Sowell on that *unconstrained* vision: ". . . [F]alsehood and force become not merely rights but duties, for the enormous benefits of an irreversible breakthrough go on for centuries, over which time the initial costs are to be amortized."[49]

In other words, the end justifies the means. This may not be what all elitists believe, but it's what's behind smear campaigns: the certainty that a brutish lie is justified by the need to move history toward its inevitable rendezvous with a rationally constructed world—constructed in the image of the elite with elitists running the show. I suspect Prof. Sowell agrees with the words of the great Edmund Burke, written more than two hundred years ago: "I have never yet seen any plan which has not been mended by the observation of those who were much inferior in understanding to the person who took the lead in the business."[50]

In *The Uncivil War*, author-attorney David Lebedoff writes that this elite—a "new educated class"—has given up on democracy, on majority rule. "Consciously or not, the New Elite has in myriad ways, by changes in rules and attitudes, already undermined and dismantled the structure of our democracy. The belief in and the capacity for self-governance daily become more eroded."[51]

Both Lebedoff and Sowell brilliantly analyze the same reality but from different points of view, and Lebedoff's is a sort of "pox-on-both-your-houses" book (primarily because it is exclusively about contemporary partisan politics), as to an extent is the one you're reading now. Looking at what empowers someone to bare fangs at a political opponent, both would see the enthusiasm of an unconstrained elitist. Democrat or Republican, liberal or conservative—these labels matter less than the elitist's utter certainty that he possesses the way and the truth and the light.

In the end we say to them all—after Oliver Cromwell—"I beseech you, in the bowels of Christ, think it possible you may be mistaken."

Fat chance.

Again, in assessing smears, smear tactics, and smear merchants, we must consider what's lurking behind the short-term political advantage being sought. Is it an electoral victory? If so, then we'll hope the smear fails—even if we lean, politically, toward the perpetrator. Win or lose, life goes on as always. Or is the goal a nation remade according to some elitist worldview? If so, we may greet those tactics with greater alarm.

This latter is the Left's aspiration. And, yes, there is a difference between their smears and the Right's*—an imbalance, and it is this: Throughout the 20th century (and so far in this one), the Left has had the media power and the academic muscle to make their smears indelible; whereas similar incivility on the Right has tended to be viewed as wackiness, the viewing after all being done through the lens of liberal media.

---

*It may be worth noting here that the largely liberal media are convinced that conservatives (and Republicans) resort to smears more readily and more often than do liberals (and Democrats). As far as I know there is no periodical survey to which one might go to check the assertion one way or another, but it is probably the case that this is assumed to be true because conservatives are assumed to be less tolerant, more rigid, and less generous than liberals. Various sources now demonstrate the assumption to be false, most notably the new book by Arthur C. Brooks of Syracuse University, *Who Really Cares: The Surprising Truth About Compassionate Conservatism* (New York: Basic Books, 2006).

Let's end this introductory chapter by considering one of the most egregious smears in recent memory—one that perfectly captures this sense of leftist desperation about the failure of the democratic process to achieve the Mandarins' ends: the smear that George W. Bush is a fascist—another Hitler.

American Holocaust?

Just so we understand, here's a brief summary (from *National Review's* Jonah Goldberg) of who the Nazis were; of what fascism is:

> Nazis murdered millions of unarmed people. They put them in ovens. They made soap out of them. They carted off children in boxcars to die and used some of the kids for medical experiments, including injecting dyes into their eyes to see if they could improve their looks. Lower on the list of charges, the Nazis enslaved millions and launched wars for territorial and egotistical gain (and sent many of the conquered populations to death camps as well). Lower still, they banned books and burned them too. They expropriated homes and businesses, banned religions, etc.[52]

Goldberg made his observation in the context of demonstrating that in some "supposedly sophisticated circles in America today it is acceptable to say George Bush is akin to a Nazi and that America is becoming Nazi-like."

Insults are not usually smears—thus we refer to smear campaigns but never speak of insult campaigns—but some insults may rise to the level of a smear—never more so than whenever some on the Left have referred to President Bush and others in his party as "fascists." That's not merely an insult, like "idiots" or even "fools"; that's a smear.

Some examples:

Aaron McGruder, creator of the "Boondocks" comic strip, has one of his characters observe: "Some people in other countries are comparing Bush to Adolf Hitler because of his warmongering." Another character replies: "That's preposterous; even I wouldn't compare him to Hitler. I mean, Hitler was democratically elected. Wasn't he?"[53]

Similarly, in February 2007 MSNBC's Chris Matthews was interviewing former New York GOP congresswoman Susan Molinari about the presidential candidacy of Rudolph Giuliani, agreeing with her that as mayor of New York City, Giuliani had done much to clean up the town. But, Matthews, wondered, "Was he a little bit of a Fascist?"

One allegation that has gained a foothold on the Left is that the razor-thin margin of the 2000 election, the outcome of which was to an extent decided in the Supreme Court, was the result of some kind of GOP putsch. Who didn't see at least one bumper sticker in 2004 that read: Re-Defeat Bush? And columnist Harvey Wasserman was only one of those who took the thought several steps further:

Few Americans believe the Bush Administration itself brought down the World Trade Center last year. But the conviction is widespread throughout Europe and the Muslim world, and for good reason. This unelected regime— Hitler also came to power with a minority of votes—has used the terrible tragedies of September 11 in much the way the Nazis jumped on the Reichstag fire.[54]

Rep. Charles Rangel, whom we met earlier in this chapter, is a critic of the Bush administration's policies with regard to the Iraq war. Fine. That's his privilege in a free society (and even his responsibility as a member of the "loyal opposition"). But when he says those policies amount to an American Holocaust, he has tipped over into smear tactics. Speaking in a radio interview, Rangel said: "[The war's] the biggest fraud ever committed on the people of this country. This is just as bad as six million Jews being killed." He then told interviewer Steve Malzberg that he is convinced Mr. Bush made up his mind to attack Iraq "long before" the terrorist attacks of September 11, 2001.[55]

And this brings us to Rosie O'Donnell and the end of this introductory chapter.

O'Donnell has used her presence on television to smear Christians as fascists, to call President Bush a war criminal, and to claim that 9/11 was an "inside job"—that, in other words, it was an American version of the Reichstag Fire, the February 27, 1933, incident in which the torching of a government building gave impetus to Hitler's seizure of dictatorial powers in Germany. O'Donnell has claimed that the collapse of World Trade Center 7 (which was not hit by either plane on 9/11) was "impossible"— that it was "the first time in history that fire has ever melted steel."[56] Her implication is that WTC7 was blown up intentionally by Americans. According to the Media Research Center, she has even suggested that Rudy Giuliani made "sure that all of the steel was removed and shipped to Canada right away" in order to hide evidence of the explosions that really brought down WTC7.[57] Her views have been thoroughly discredited scientifically in *Popular Mechanics* and elsewhere, and no sensible person really believes that al Qaeda wasn't behind the attacks or that President Bush was—but to the Left the smear is sufficient because it enhances the aura of sinister fascism about the commander in chief.

And one may wonder if it matters what Rosie O'Donnell thinks and says—if she has any influence at all. Well, there must be some reason that *TIME* magazine named her one of its 100 most influential people, and why a Rasmussen Reports poll recently indicated that 35 percent of Democrats believe Mr. Bush knew of the 9/11 attacks in advance![58]

This is not some "lunatic fringe" and, as we shall see, it has more often than not been the case that smears stick like a sort of stinking cement to the targets of attack even after they've been revealed to be false.

Let's consider, then, some big smears; some lies and rumors that have not only cut deep those at whom they have been aimed but that have kept cutting long after—in some case even after the truth has been revealed and the smear apparently refuted. J. Edgar Hoover was a cross-dresser, right? General William Westmoreland cooked the books in Vietnam, right? Many of America's religious leaders are no different from Iranian ayatollahs, right? The millions of voters who reelected George W. Bush are stupid and evil, no?

Is there any end to the bad-mouthing?

II

SMEARING PATRIOTS

My daughter, who goes to Stuyvesant High School only blocks from the World Trade Center, thinks we should fly an American flag out our window. Definitely not, I say: The flag stands for jingoism and vengeance and war.
　　　　　　　　　—Left-wing journalist Katha Pollitt, after 9/11[1]

IT MAY BE THAT THE MOST famous statement ever made about patriotism was Dr. Samuel Johnson's dismissive quip (an apothegm recorded by James Boswell in his *Life of Johnson*) that it is "the last refuge of the scoundrel." Trouble is, Dr. Johnson's observation—evoked by people of all political persuasions—was more about scoundrels than about patriots. He was referring to the sort of political criminals who wrap themselves in a flag the way frightened boys duck behind their mothers' skirts. As Boswell explained, Johnson "did not mean a real and generous love of our country, but that pretended patriotism which so many, in all ages and countries, have made a cloak for self-interest."[2] That's pretty much what the Dixie Chicks, the country-music group, have been accusing American patriots of doing.

The controversy began in March 2003, when the Chicks, who are from Texas, were on a European tour. At a concert in London, lead singer Natalie Maines told the audience, "Just so you know, we're ashamed the president of the United States is from Texas. We do not want war."[3]

Later that week, she amplified on her comments: "I feel the president is ignoring the opinion of many in the U.S. and alienating the rest of the world. My comments were made in frustration, and one of the privileges of being an American is you are free to voice your own point of view."[4]

Back home, the outrage was palpable. "It was like the McCarthy days, and it was almost like the country was unrecognizable," said Maines's band mate, Emily Robinson, and the Chicks expressed shock at the extent to which other country-music performers refused to support them. Other artists even did patriotic songs and videos, which the Chicks considered pure exploitation of the reaction to Maines's comment about President Bush. Robinson told the London *Telegraph*: "A lot of pandering started going on, and you'd see soldiers and the American flag in every video. It became a sickening display of ultra-patriotism."[5]

What is the difference between patriotism and its "ultra" variety? Perhaps none, as Maines seemed to indicate in her interview for the same *Telegraph* article.

> "The entire country may disagree with me, but I don't understand the necessity for patriotism," Maines resumes, through gritted teeth. "Why do you have to be a patriot? About what? This land is our land? Why? You can like where you live and like your life, but as for loving the whole country . . . I don't see why people care about patriotism."

Let's see if we can see why many people *do care* about patriotism—and what the consequences might be of abandoning it.

Why Be Patriotic?

As Adlai Stevenson once put it, to say an American is patriotic is to say "not only that he loves the New England hills, the prairies glistening in the sun, the wide and rising plains, the great mountains, and the sea. He means that he loves an inner air, an inner light in which freedom lives and in which a man can draw the breath of self-respect."[6]

It is that and more. Edmund Burke, the great English founder of modern conservatism, observed that each of us is led to patriotism first through love of family and community. "To love the little platoon we belong to in society," he wrote, "is the first principle of public affections. It is the first link in the series by which we proceed towards a love to our country and to mankind."[7]

By contrast the American Left—ever since, roughly speaking, the mid-1960s—has shown every sign of hating America and every eagerness to destroy its living traditions. The Vietnam War provided the impetus, or at least the excuse, for many Americans to say their country was not worth dying for—or fit to live in. As scruffy demonstrators on the streets shouted "Hey, hey, LBJ, how many kids did you kill today?" their tenured elders on the campuses were telling them that American society was irremediably bad. Here is the guru of the New Left, Herbert Marcuse, professor of philosophy and politics at the University of California/San Diego:

> I have tried to show that contemporary society is a repressive society in all its aspects. . . . I have tried to show that any change would require a total rejection . . . of this society. . . . I have been accused of concentrating my critique on American society, and this is quite true. . . . The students have said

that they are opposing the violence of society, legal violence, institutional violence. Their violence is that of defense. They have said this, and I believe it is true. . . . The students have said it: a revolution is always just as violent as the violence it combats. I believe they are right.[8]

At the same time, Noam Chomsky, professor of linguistics at MIT, was saying: "Our military effort in Vietnam is a revolting and disgusting barbarism. . . . The Pentagon is the most hideous institution on this earth, and the United States stands convicted of unconstrainted viciousness and butchery."[9]

The Left's enmity toward America was tied to its enmity toward "repressive, racist, patriarchal" Western civilization. A generation after the "Hey, hey, LBJ" chant, students at Stanford University, led by visiting preacher Jesse Jackson, were chanting, "Hey, hey, ho, ho, Western Culture's got to go." Western Culture was the basic course at Stanford that taught "the canon"—i.e., the best of the Dead White Males, from Plato to Mill. In New York State, Commissioner of Education Thomas Sobol ordered a revamping of the public-school curriculum. The resulting report, "A Curriculum of Inclusion," began: "African Americans, Asian Americans, Puerto Ricans/Latinos, and Native Americans have all been the victims of an intellectual and educational oppression that has characterized the culture and institutions of the United States and the European American world for centuries."[10]

Why Do They Hate Us?

In the aftermath of September 11, 2001, liberals and hard-core leftists took to the presses and the airwaves with what to them was a heartfelt question: *Why do they hate us?*—"they" being either the terrorists specifically or Islamists more generally, depending upon just how far left the questioner was. It took several weeks for the few Americans who actually did express sympathy for al Qaeda to do so publicly. And, in truth, most liberals had no empathy at all for the terrorists—then or now.

Few conservatives or moderates posed that question, and when they did, they had an answer in mind like the one given editorially by *National Review*: "The United States is a target because we are powerful, rich, and good. We are resented for our power, envied for our wealth, and hated for our liberty." [11]* But most of us didn't care *why* they hate us; we simply wanted to know who the criminals were, where they were, and how we could bring them to justice. And in the "wanted-dead-or-alive" calculus, we definitely preferred dead.

Why do they hate us? The question hung in the air like acrid smoke, and those who asked it seemed to be implying something more. *What can we do to make them like us?* That was the bleeding-heart liberal's cri de coeur. *How can you blame them?* That was the hard-core leftist's heartless query. In both cases, there was the implication—I should say, there *is* the implication—that the

---

*An exception may be Dinesh D'Souza, in his controversial book *The Enemy at Home: The Cultural Left and Its Responsibility for 9/11* (Doubleday, 2007). Writing in *Booklist*, Vanessa Bush summed up D'Souza's argument: "The cultural Left in the U.S., by pressing for sexual freedom for women and gays through birth control, no-fault divorce, and support for gay marriage, has not only undermined American culture but also provoked the ire of religious conservatives in other nations, most prominently Islamic fundamentalists. Contrary to President Bush's assertions that terrorists and their supporters hate American freedom, D'Souza asserts that what they really hate is our licentious culture. He notes that American conservatives have more in common with Islamic fundamentalists than with American liberals." But his was indeed a lonely voice.

United States of America was the aggressor. If the liberals hoped America would confess her sins, and the hard leftists that the nation would be punished still more, scarcely mattered to the basic answer; in each case, the horrid fundamental assumption was that we, somehow, had caused the attack.

The looniest of the loony even suggested that the Bush administration—also known as "Bushitler," that all-purpose bugaboo of the Left (and also, it must be said, of the radical libertarian Right), the like of which has not existed since the "International Jewish Conspiracy" first gained traction in the *Protocols of the Elders of Zion*—engineered the attacks on the World Trade Center, in order to gain an excuse to attack Afghanistan. The goal: cheap oil. Others claim that the Israelis either directed, or knew of and did nothing to prevent, the attacks, in order to shore up American hatred for Muslims and therefore support of Israel; or that there never were any planes or hijackers at all: the buildings were blown up from the inside. Some of the rants are to be found in creases in the fabric of the Internet; others are right out there stating their opinions on CNN, or in the pages of the *New York Times*, or in front of eager undergraduates at Columbia University. The sum of those opinions is this: the genesis of 9/11 is American patriotism, and the true villains of that day aren't Osama bin Laden and his henchmen but the people who believe America is the greatest nation on the face of the earth. And, as we review the smears made against patriots, remember this: there are few places in the world where such slanders would be tolerated. The smear mongers depend on it.

The most famous of these smears, probably, is the one by Ward Churchill, professor of ethnic studies at the University of Colorado at Boulder. In his essay "Some People Push Back," apparently written on 9/11 itself, Churchill said:

When queried by reporters concerning his views on the assassination of John F. Kennedy in November 1963, Malcolm X famously—and quite charitably, all things considered—replied that it was merely a case of "chickens coming home to roost."

On the morning of September 11, 2001, a few more chickens—along with some half-million dead Iraqi children—came home to roost in a very big way at the twin towers of New York's World Trade Center. Well, actually, a few of them seem to have nestled in at the Pentagon as well. . . .

The most that can honestly be said of those involved on September 11 is that they finally responded in kind to some of what this country has dispensed to their people as a matter of course. That they waited so long to do so is, notwithstanding the 1993 action at the WTC, more than anything a testament to their patience and restraint.

They did not license themselves to "target innocent civilians."

There is simply no argument to be made that the Pentagon personnel killed on September 11 fill that bill. The building and those inside comprised military targets, pure and simple. As to those in the World Trade Center . . . Well, really. Let's get a grip here, shall we? True enough, they were civilians of a sort. But innocent? Gimme a break. They formed a technocratic corps at the very heart of America's global financial empire—the "mighty engine of profit" to which the military dimension of U.S. policy has always been enslaved—and they did so both willingly and knowingly. Recourse to "ignorance"— a derivative, after all, of the word "ignore"—counts as less than an excuse among this relatively well-educated elite. To the extent that any of them were unaware of the costs and consequences to others of what they were involved in—and in many cases excelling at—it was because of their absolute refusal to see. More likely, it was because they were too busy braying, incessantly and self-importantly, into their cell phones, arranging power lunches and stock transactions, each of which translated, conveniently out of sight, mind and smelling distance, into the starved and rotting flesh of infants. If there was a better, more effective, or in fact any other way of visiting some penalty befitting their participation upon the little Eichmanns inhabiting the sterile sanctuary of the twin towers, I'd really be interested in hearing about it.[12]

Susan Sontag also famously weighed in, in *The New Yorker*'s "Talk of the Town":

The disconnect between last Tuesday's monstrous dose of reality and the self-righteous drivel and outright deceptions being peddled by public figures and TV commentators is startling, depressing. The voices licensed to follow the event seem to have joined together in a campaign to infantilize the public. Where is the acknowledgment that this was not a "cowardly" attack on "civilization" or "liberty" or "humanity" or "the free world" but an attack on the world's self-proclaimed superpower, undertaken as a consequence of specific American alliances and actions? How many citizens are aware of the ongoing American bombing of Iraq?[13]

Morgan Reynolds, who once worked in the Bush administration but is now allied with libertarian Lew Rockwell, spends several thousand words explicating his theory that the destruction of the World Trade Center was an "inside job." His opening and closing arguments read as follows:

> To explain the unanticipated free-fall collapses of the twin towers at the World Trade Center on September 11, 2001, mainstream experts . . . offer a three-stage argument: 1) an airplane impact weakened each structure, 2) an intense fire thermally weakened structural components that may have suffered damage to fireproofing materials, causing buckling failures, which, in turn, 3) allowed the upper floors to pancake onto the floors below.
>
> Many will nod their head, OK, that does it, and go back to watching the NBA finals or whatever, but I find this theory just about as satisfying as the fantastic conspiracy theory that "19 young Arabs acting at the behest of Islamist extremists headquartered in distant Afghanistan" caused 9/11. The government's collapse theory is highly vulnerable on its own terms, but its blinkered narrowness and lack of breadth is the paramount defect unshared by its principal scientific rival—controlled demolition. Only professional demolition appears to account for the full range of facts associated with the collapses of WTC 1 (North Tower), WTC 2 (South Tower), and the much-overlooked collapse of the 47-story WTC building 7 at 5:21 pm on that fateful day. . . .
>
> . . . momentous political and social consequences would follow if impartial observers concluded that professionals imploded the WTC. If demolition destroyed three steel skyscrapers at the World Trade Center on 9/11, then the case for an "inside job" and a government attack on America would be compelling.[14]

Two other authors, Richard Stanley and Jerry Russell, took the same approach to the 9/11 attack on the Pentagon:

> Earliest reports from the Pentagon indicated that a helicopter explosion or attack took place. However, during the course of the day, two legends were put into place—the first, that the Pentagon was struck by an airliner; and also an alternative hoax, that a missile was responsible. But no tangible, verifiable evidence of an airliner crash at the Pentagon has ever been produced. Our analysis indicates that in reality, sophisticated shaped-charge explosive technology was used to create a scene comporting with the appearance of a jetliner crash, while simultaneously a 757 over flew the area and landed at nearby Reagan National Airport. If this scenario is correct, it shows that US intelligence agencies have developed an extraordinary capability to create elaborate magic shows on the world stage, generate false testimony and false evidence, and control and manipulate not only the "official story" but also its dialectical opposition among the critics.[15]

As for United Flight 93, which crashed into that field in Pennsylvania, well—"Looking at all the details so far—nothing really adds up neatly for me, except that Flight 93 had a midair crisis that caused debris to fall before it crashed. I remain skeptical of all the theories . . . except one. We are not being told what happened—and the Government knows exactly what happened."[16]

The theory that it was not our government but Ariel Sharon's that knew first circulated in the Arab press in the Middle East; its most prominent upholder in our country was New Jersey's poet laureate, Amiri Baraka (some will remember him from the sixties as "black cultural nationalist" LeRoi Jones). In his 9/11 poem, "Somebody Blew Up America," he wrote:

> *Who knew the World Trade Center was gonna get*
> *bombed?*
> *Who told 4,000 Israeli workers at the Twin Towers*
> *To stay home that day?*
> *Why did Sharon stay away?*[17]

In March 2003, the Columbia Anti-War Coalition organized a six-hour "teach-in," in which three dozen leading faculty members denounced the Bush administration's plans to invade Iraq. Many of the speakers made a point of the controversy over the 2000 election. Journalism professor Todd Gitlin contended that George Bush's "coup d'état" was what led us to the brink of war. English professor Bruce Robbins described the administration as an "un-elected government" run by "shameless liars and hypocrites" who have "no respect for the rule of law." History professor Barbara Fields accused Bush's cabinet members of being "tyrants who have ignored the consent of the governed." International Affairs professor Roger Normand equated Donald Rumsfeld with Hitler's second in command, Hermann Goering. But the star of the show was Nicholas De Genova, professor of anthropology and Latin American studies, who proclaimed: "Peace is not patriotic. Peace is subversive, because peace anticipates a very different world than the one in which we live—a world where the U.S. would have no place. . . . U.S. patriotism is inseparable from imperial warfare and white supremacy."[18]

Professor miriam cooke (yes, she writes her name in lower-case), like Professor Churchill, looks for the source of September 11 in the policies of the West and, especially, the United States:

> War, war machines, jihad. These words have entered the vocabulary of everyday practice during the past twenty years. They mark a new stage in the discourse of Empire, what Hardt and Negri call a global project of network power, that knits the world together in a dynamic fabric of exchange, flows but also of conflict.
>
> 9-11 was a catastrophic example of the ways in which the threads in this fabric tighten and break. American citizens felt for the first time how the apparently innocent business of moneymaking in New York City and of policymaking in Washington DC are seen as criminal elsewhere. The daily deals struck in the financial and military-political capitals of the U.S. have direct and mostly negative consequences for most of the rest of the world. These consequences are invisible to Joe 6-pack, they are searingly obvious elsewhere.
>
> 9-11 has a long history going back through the Gulf War to the establishment of Israel in 1948. It is a history that spans the length of the Cold War and is witness to the growing suspicion and fear of U.S. policies in the region. Indeed, the last great battle of the Cold War took place in a dry dusty landlocked backwater called Afghanistan. Having been chosen for this showdown between the two superpowers placed Afghanistan squarely on the stage of world history.[19]

Her essay, "War, Its Machines and the Women Who Fight Them," was published in prestigious Duke University's *Faculty Viewpoints* and offers a glimpse of the kind of intemperate, subjective, rambling screed that is tolerated under the aegis of academic freedom.

And the Beat Goes On

The smearing didn't stop with 9/11 itself. Singer Harry Belafonte, in a speech to the annual meeting of the Arts Presenters Members Conference in 2006, said, "We've come to this dark time in which the new Gestapo lurks here, where citizens are having their rights suspended."[20]

On CNN, Wolf Blitzer asked Mr. Belafonte whether he could really defend his characterization of the Department of Homeland Security as equivalent to the principal agency of Nazi terror. The erstwhile calypso singer replied, "I stand by my remarks. I am very much aware of what this has provoked in our national community, and I welcome the opportunity for us to begin to have a dialogue, that goes other than where we have been having one up until now."[21]

Belafonte seems to be aping the philosophy of Marx—the revolutionary process of thesis-antithesis-synthesis, otherwise known as "dialectical evolution." This is the problem of communitarian consensus: if we begin with two premises, and the goal is a synthesis of the two, we are driven by both regardless of whether one is utterly erroneous. What exactly is the synthesis of good and evil?

Coulterkampf

Conservative columnist and author Ann Coulter, whatever else she may be, is a patriot. And she is a lightning rod for liberal attacks—nearly as much as George W. Bush. She is, as the phrase has it, a woman they "love to hate." (*Late Show* host David Letterman quipped that former vice president Al Gore had made a follow-up documentary to his successful *An Inconvenient Truth*, this one about Miss Coulter. "I believe it's called *An Inconvenient Bitch*.")

The latest battle involving Miss Coulter stems from statements she made about four widows of men who died on 9/11. These women, the self-styled Jersey Girls (Kristen Breitweiser, Lorie Van Auken, Mindy Kleinberg, and Patty Casazza), had criticized President Bush, his administration, and the U.S. intelligence services for not preventing the 9/11 attacks. They demanded answers to their questions and pushed, successfully, for the creation of the 9/11 Commission. In her controversial best seller *Godless: The Church of Liberalism*, Coulter wrote:

> These self-obsessed women seemed genuinely unaware that 9/11 was an attack on our nation and acted as if the terrorist attacks happened only to them. The whole nation was wounded, all of our lives reduced. But they believed the entire country was required to marinate in their exquisite personal agony. Apparently, denouncing Bush was an important part of their closure process. These broads are millionaires, lionized on TV and in articles about them, reveling in their status as celebrities and stalked by grief-arazzis. I've never seen people enjoying their husbands' deaths so much.[22]

Coulter quickly found herself under fire. Sen. Hillary Rodham Clinton called her comments "vicious" and "mean-spirited," and the Jersey Girls themselves issued a statement that read in part: "We have been slandered. Contrary to Ms. Coulter's statements, there was no joy in watching men that we loved burn alive. There was no happiness in telling our children that their fathers were never coming home again. We adored these men and miss them every day."[23]

This seems heartfelt, though it doesn't answer Coulter's point that "They have attacked Bush, they have attacked Condoleezza Rice, they're cutting campaign commercials for Kerry. But we can't respond because their husbands died. . . . I think it's one of the ugliest things the left has done to political dialogue in this country—this idea that you need some sort of personal authenticity in order to make a political point. . . ."[24]

Ann Coulter wasn't the only person to question the Jersey Girls' politics or their passion for publicity. As Dorothy Rabinowitz wrote in the *Wall Street Journal*, despite Mrs. Breitweiser's earlier complaints that the media were ignoring them, the Girls were all over TV once the 9/11 Commission began meeting:

> Others who had lost family to the terrorists' assault commanded little to no interest from TV interviewers. Debra Burlingame—lifelong Democrat, sister of Charles F. "Chic" Burlingame III, captain of American Airlines flight 77, which crashed into the Pentagon on Sept. 11, did manage to land an interview. . . . When she had finished airing her views critical of the accusatory tone and tactics of the Jersey Girls, her interviewer, ABC congressional reporter Linda Douglass, marveled, "This is the first time I've heard this point of view."[25]

(In the interest of full disclosure, I should state that both Miss Coulter and Ms. Burlingame are acquaintances of mine.)

Coulter also dubbed the "weeping widows" the "Witches of East Brunswick," a parody of the title of a John Updike novel.

Ann Coulter has been attacked by the Left ever since she first began writing, and especially after the publication of her first book, *High Crimes and Misdemeanors* (Regnery Publishing, 1998), in which she laid out the case for impeaching President Bill Clinton. To say that she is not shy about expressing her opinions is an understatement, and it also seems safe to say she often frames her arguments in the most provocative way possible. Thus, when describing liberals in her book *Treason* (Crown Forum, 2003), she says they are "savagely cruel bigots who hate ordinary Americans and lie for sport." Coulter tends to bring out the worst in her opponents, which is why she is usually more smeared than smearer.

Three recent books have attacked her, specifically in terms of the issues raised in *Godless*. The most remarkable is *Soulless: Ann Coulter and the Right-Wing Church of Hate*, by Susan Estrich;[26] less so are *Brainless: The Lies and Lunacy of Ann Coulter*, by Joe Maguire,[27] and *I Hate Ann Coulter!*, by Unanimous.[28]

Estrich's book (whose cover is a down-to-the-smallest-detail parody of *Godless*) begins:

Welcome to Ann's world. And what a mean and nasty world it is. Here she is taking all the decent impulses that make Americans compassionate, hopeful, and generous—real Liberalism—and, with a total disregard for history and humanity, twisting them into the opposite of what they are.

How does she do it? An ounce of sophistry, a touch of misrepresentation, lit up with invective and some sly wit.

But she doesn't do it alone. Not even close.

She does it by using a media that's obsessed with entertainment. For them, long, blond, svelte Ann is the cutely packaged girl next door (if next door is Darien, Connecticut) who can impress the college boys by being able to talk dirty and nasty with the best of them. Venom is what she spills.

Estrich's text is an attempt—with liberal quoting of Coulter's text—to refute, point by point, the assertions made in *Godless*. The book is passionate, although rather too much so for its own good. For instance, Estrich refers to "Reverend [James] Dobson's Focus on the Family," but Dr. Dobson is not an ordained minister; he's a psychologist.[29] Of the Paula Jones scandal—in which Miss Jones alleged sexual harassment by Bill Clinton while he was governor of Arkansas and in which Ann Coulter, an attorney (like Miss Estrich), played a role—Estrich writes that the case was dismissed as being without merit. In fact, what Judge Susan Wheeler Wright ruled was that Miss Jones had not legally demonstrated any damages requiring monetary compensation. (During an appeal of Wright's ruling, President Clinton made an out-of-court settlement with Jones for $850,000. Mr. Clinton was also found guilty—by Judge Wright—of civil contempt, which led to a five-year suspension of his license to practice law.)

Maguire's *Brainless* is a shorter, less ambitious attempt to mount a "full-frontal assault on her methods, her mischief, and her madness," although Maguire insists that it is not an "attack on Ann Coulter the person." However, in his first chapter he writes:

The arguments she makes are misleading to the point of being outright lies. On top of that, they're often irrelevant and typically directed at people rather than positions.

Normally, in the face of such blather, I'd move on and try to find something a bit more reasonable. But it's hard to ignore someone who tosses around words like "harpies" and "raghead" . . . Ann Coulter is absolutely right when she says that "arguments by demonization . . . can be presumed to be fraudulent." Which kind of casts a shadow over . . . oh . . . *just about everything she's ever written.*

Just to look at one example of Maguire's method, he takes Coulter to task for suggesting that there is no scientific basis for the lawsuits that claim breast implants cause serious health problems. He says her assertion is "an outright lie." No doubt arguments can be made on both sides of the safety issue with regard to implants, but it seems reasonable to note that nearly all studies since the 1990s have been unable to find any link between implants and the litany of illnesses attributed to them.[30] Specifically, studies by Britain's Independent Expert Advisory Group, France's *Agence Nationale pour le Développement de l'Evaluation Medicale*, Australia's Therapeutic Devices Evaluation Committee, Germany's Federal Institute for Drugs and Medical Products, the European Union's Committee on Quality Assurance and Medical Devices in Plastic Surgery, and both the Institute of Medicine and the National Science Panel in the USA seem to document fairly well Ann Coulter's objections to costly implant lawsuits, and to call into question the temper of Maguire's characterization of her objections as *outright lies.*

As for *I Hate Ann Coulter!* . . . Well, it's the sort of book that ought to have stimulated its publisher's better instincts. The four authors of the book rehash the liberal media meme that Coulter is a liar and a fool, but they do it in a way that raises it to the level of a smear: "SHE SAYS: 'It's no fun riding around in those dinky little hybrid cars.' WE SAY: Ann, think of it as a mode of transportation, not as an extension of your penis."

It's not my intention here to highlight the many vices and few virtues of *Brainless* or *Soulless* or *I Hate Ann Coulter!* or, for that matter, *Godless*. Rather it is to point out a fundamental misconception most foes and even some friends have about Ann Coulter. What Coulter's critics fail to understand (and—although it may be impertinent of me to suggest it—Ann *herself* sometimes fails to grasp) is that she is principally a satirist. I won't say she's a satirist "pure and simple," because much of what she says and writes is quite straightforward—more-or-less well-researched observations of America's current political environment. She's a brilliant woman who carefully considers most of what she writes and says.

But the fact remains: She is to the 21st century what Lenny Bruce was to the 20th, a truly outrageous social commentator attempting to make people reexamine basic assumptions.

Leftists will swoon at a comparison of Coulter and the sainted Bruce. They will object that Lenny was the scourge of the reigning orthodoxies of the fifties and sixties, whereas Ann is the herald of our contemporary Establishment. But this is untrue. Bruce was all that, but Coulter is the angry voice of American tradition, lashing out at a *New* Establishment (or, better, a New *Disestablishment*) and the reigning heterodoxy of the media and the universities and the law that is laying siege to that tradition. And I'm not alone in thinking this. In an article in the *Wall Street Journal* ("Dr. Johnson, Meet Ann Coulter!"), Melik Kaylan wrote:

We have been programmed to think that such impassioned outrage, and outrageousness, are permissible only on the left, from counter-culture comedians or exponents of identity politics, certainly not from nice blonde Connecticut-born Republican girls. From Lenny Bruce, George Carlin, Angela Davis, Reverend Farrakhan, yes. Ann Coulter—heaven forbid.[31]

But with all this, we cannot present Miss Coulter as merely a victim of liberal reaction to her quick wit.

In Chapter 1, I suggested that, whereas a smear needs to be distinguished from an insult, some insults *do* rise to the level of smears, and I gave as an example the use by many on the Left of the word "fascist" to describe some conservatives, and especially George W. Bush. (We'll remain for a moment agnostic on the question of whether or not Mr. Bush actually is a conservative.) But "fascist" isn't the only one-word smear; "faggot" is another, and that brings us back to Miss Coulter.

In March 2007, in a speech at the Conservative Political Action Conference (CPAC), Coulter made an allusion to the travails of the actor Isaiah Washington, who had got himself in hot water—and into counseling—for calling T. R. Knight, another cast member of TV's *Grey's Anatomy*, a "faggot," an extremely unpleasant reference to his homosexuality. At CPAC, Miss Coulter used the same term in reference to Sen. John Edwards, a married father of four. She said, "I was going to have a few comments on the other presidential candidate, John Edwards, but it turns out you have to go into rehab if you use the word "faggot," so I—so kind of an impasse, can't really talk about Edwards."[32]

Perhaps what she meant was that she considers Edwards to be weak; perhaps, in other words, she meant what Gov. Arnold Schwarzenegger of California meant when he referred to state

legislators whom he considered timid as "girlie men." But Arnold
was making (partly) a self-deprecating joke based on the parody
of him done on *Saturday Night Live* by Dana Carvey and Kevin
Nealon (Hans and Franz, respectively), whereas Ann's quip, although it almost certainly wasn't meant to suggest that Sen. Edwards has a secret life akin to that of former New Jersey governor
Jim McGreevey, was clearly offensive and, under the circumstances, a smear. As a group of conservatives and libertarians put
it in "An Open Letter to CPAC Sponsors and Organizers Regarding Ann Coulter": "Coulter's vicious word choice tells the
world she cares little about the feelings of a large group that often
feels marginalized and despised. Her word choice forces conservatives to waste time defending themselves against charges of ho-
mophobia rather than advancing conservative ideas."[33]

It is interesting that the concern of the people who signed the
letter is for gays as a group rather than Sen. Edwards as an individual, but it is certainly the case, as they also wrote, that it is
tough to "teach young conservatives to fight for their principles
with civility and respect" when Ann Coulter, considered by many
a conservative leader, seems disinclined to treat opponents with
either civility or respect.

For her part, Coulter was wistful. "C'mon, it was a joke," she
wrote in an e-mail. "I would never insult gays by suggesting they
are like John Edwards. That would be mean."[34] As I wrote earlier:
Lenny Bruce.

A Feather Boa?

Which reminds me that if I were asked if I have a "favorite" smear
(if it's appropriate—or even possible—to say one has a favorite

among this obnoxious category), I'd have to choose one of the American Left's most vicious urban legends, namely that J. Edgar Hoover—a patriot if he was nothing else—was a transvestite.

You've almost certainly heard the rumor that the most famous G-Man of them all liked to wear "a fluffy black dress, very fluffy, with flounces and lace stockings and high heels, and a black curly wig."[35] And makeup and false eyelashes, too.

Is there any truth to this? Well, the source of the accusations just quoted is one Susan Rosenstiel, who told stories of several times seeing Hoover in dresses to pop biographer Anthony Summers, author also of books about other "fallen" men: Richard Nixon, John F. Kennedy, Frank Sinatra, and Czar Nicholas II (and one fallen *Goddess*, Marilyn Monroe). A number of more temperate observers have termed these tales rubbish. It may be a source of hilarity for some to imagine the head of the FBI at New York's Plaza Hotel, "wearing a red dress . . . Around his neck was a black feather boa. He was holding a Bible, and he asked [a] . . . blond [boy] to read a passage as another boy played with him," but how likely is it?

As we were taught in logic class, it is impossible to prove a negative. However, we are allowed to deploy common sense, as veteran journalist Ronald Kessler does in his book *The FBI*: "The director of the FBI simply could not have engaged in such activity at the Plaza, with a number of witnesses present, without having it leak out. . . . [Yet that] Hoover was a cross-dresser is now largely presumed to be fact even by sophisticated people."[36]

More recently, Michael Binyon, veteran editorial writer of *The Times* of London, learned from KGB defector Vasili Mitrokhin—none of whose information has been disproved—that the Hoover-was-a-cross-dresser smear was assiduously cultivated by none other than the KGB. Binyon writes:

America was the top target for most KGB operations, but most were dirty tricks that were often as crude as they were farcical. . . .

Among the more successful was an attempt to throw suspicion on the CIA for involvement in the assassination of President Kennedy, the allegation that Martin Luther King was in the pay of President Johnson and the assiduous cultivation of rumours that J. Edgar Hoover, the veteran head of the FBI, was a closet homosexual and cross-dresser.[37]

But Mitrokhin's revelation—previously locked away in files in the Lubyanka—has done little to diminish the allure of the smear.

Unscrupulous activists on the Left can make much mischief by smearing deceased public figures such as Hoover or New York's Cardinal Spellman with the charge that they were gay. What is especially repugnant is that the accusers are often gay themselves, as is the case with journalist and talk show host Michelangelo Signorile, who has claimed that "the archconservative Spellman was the epitome of the self-loathing, closeted, evil queen, working with his good friend, the closeted gay McCarthy henchman Roy Cohn, to undermine liberalism in America. . . ."[38]

As evidence, Signorile cites an unpublished version of John Cooney's biography of Spellman, *The American Pope*, in which he had included unsubstantiated rumors about the Cardinal's sexuality. (Reviewers and commentators are routinely cautioned by publishers never to quote from advance proofs of a book, but to wait until it is actually published.) But as *New York Times* reviewer William Shannon wrote, in the published version Cooney "wisely abandoned his attempt to argue that Spellman was a homosexual."[39] Shannon's argument may not be strong: Essentially he argues that prurience in biography serves no purpose, and that, in any case, it doesn't matter what public people do in private. That's a fair subject for debate, but what seems clear is that Cooney chose not to include in the final version of his book material he could not confirm, and that Signorile chose to base his smear of Spellman on material that was eventually cut. He is content to employ whatever means he can to attack someone he considers evil.

Signorile's assertions are a smear because they serve only his political/social interests—which involve making homosexuality normative—and not the interests of historical truth, which in this case, as Cooney and Shannon acknowledge, demand caution.

Perhaps Signorile would argue that his distortions serve a "larger truth." Smear merchants often do.

Running Down Ronnie

As noted in the first chapter, all presidents of the United States find themselves on the business end of smear tactics by their political opponents, but—at least until Clinton and the second Bush—few commanders in chief were the target of as much enmity as Ronald Wilson Reagan.

Among the more famous put-downs of Reagan were diplomat Clark Clifford's observation that he was an "amiable dunce," and columnist Nicholas von Hoffman's complaint: "How humiliating to think of this unlettered, self-assured bumpkin being our president."[40]

But those comments were mild in comparison to some. In the aftermath of Mr. Reagan's death in June 2004, cartoonist and author Ted Rall reacted with scorn to the outpouring of affection for the late president.

Given that he made flying a living hell (by firing the air traffic controllers and regulating [sic] the airlines), I'm not the only one who refuses to call Washington National Airport by its new name. His clown-like dyed hair and rouged cheeks disgusted us. We hated him during the dark days he made so hideous, and, with all due respect, we hate him still.[41]

As the publication of his early writings and speeches has shown,* Reagan was no dunce, but he certainly was amiable, and it's hard to grasp the hatred Rall expresses. Yet it is widely shared on the Left. Here is Christopher Hitchens:

> The fox, as has been pointed out by more than one philosopher, knows many small things, whereas the hedgehog knows one big thing. Ronald Reagan was neither a fox nor a hedgehog. He was as dumb as a stump. He could have had anyone in the world to dinner, any night of the week, but took most of his meals on a White House TV tray. He had no friends, only cronies. His children didn't like him all that much. He met his second wife—the one that you remember—because she needed to get off a Hollywood blacklist and he was the man to see. Year in and year out in Washington, I could not believe that such a man had even been a poor governor of California in a bad year, let alone that such a smart country would put up with such an obvious phony and loon.[42]

*I'm thinking particularly of the series of books done by Kiron Skinner and Martin and Annelise Anderson, including: *Reagan: A Life in Letters* (Free Press, 2003); *Stories in His Own Hand: The Everyday Wisdom of Ronald Reagan* (2001); *Reagan's Path to Victory: The Shaping of Ronald Reagan's Vision* (2004); and *Reagan, In His Own Hand: The Writings of Ronald Reagan That Reveal His Revolutionary Vision for America* (2001).

And here is blogger Irene Monroe:

> Every morning during the Reagan era (1981–1989), my
> morning meditation was Psalm 23, as my prayer of protec-
> tion. It was the first half of the fourth verse I repeated con-
> stantly during those days: "Even though I walk through the
> valley of death, I will fear no evil." And while I would like to
> say I walked sure-footed during those years, I didn't.
> Throughout the Reagan years, my steps were tentative as
> I walked through my urban African-American enclave in
> New York City and witnessed folks dying from a mysterious
> virus that during its nascent stage had no name.
>   Our country's AIDS epidemic during the reign of Reagan
> caused me to revisit the theological concept that, in my
> opinion, was used too cavalierly in my Christian fundamen-
> talist growing-up years—evil. . . . [43]

Many on the Left can never forgive Mr. Reagan for firing the
air-traffic controllers during their illegal strike in 1981; calling the
Soviet Union an "evil empire" in 1983; failing to declare a national
war on AIDS (at a time when its nature was little known and
widely debated); and more generally for his advocacy of limited
government, tax cuts, and supply-side economics. The liberal Web
site SourceWatch even uses the "evil empire" phrase as one illus-
tration of a smear, which it says "led to nearly universal condemnation" of Reagan, who nonetheless "never retracted his allegation,
despite repeated requests to do so." [44]

President Reagan never retracted—or apologized—because he
did not rue the comments he had made. His self-confidence tended
to infuriate the press. In a column immediately after Reagan's

death, *Time*'s Joe Klein wrote: "Unlike other Presidents—except, perhaps, for Abraham Lincoln and Andrew Jackson—Reagan came to power as the leader of an ideological movement: in his case, a fierce conservatism forged and tempered by decades of disdain from the nation's moderate media and political establishment."[45]

The term "political establishment" is a tough one to define—and I'm not sure how Klein would define it—but the last time the nation's media were moderate was in about 1968. In any case, Klein at least recognized in Reagan an uncompromising determination on the subject of Soviet communism. He begins that column by describing the late president's face as seeming out of a wax museum, his demeanor as a "sunny opacity," his governance as "sloppy and often insensitive," and his behavior as "rote and mechanical"—all of this suggesting some kind of hollow man. But then Klein concludes by remembering a visit to the Soviet Union:

In fact, I didn't understand how truly monumental, and morally important, Reagan's anticommunist vision was until I visited the Soviet Union in 1987. My first night there, I was escorted to the Bolshoi Ballet by two minders from the U.S.-Canada Institute. The Russians were thrilled that I had figured out the Cyrillic alphabet and was able to read the program. The young woman on my left rewarded me with a smile—a rare public act in that terrifying regime—and a whispered encouragement: reform was coming. Glasnost and perestroika, she assured me, were real. The minder on my left, a chunky young man, then nudged me with his elbow. "Ronald Reagan. Evil empire," he whispered with dramatic intensity, and shot a glance down to his lap where he had hidden two enthusiastic thumbs up. "Yes!"

But if Mr. Klein only reluctantly saw the good side of Ronald Reagan and Rall couldn't see it at all, most Americans saw it clearly. Which is why there was such an outpouring of anger and protest when, in 2003, CBS began to promote its TV mini-series *The Reagans*, starring James Brolin (Barbra Streisand's husband) and Australian actress Judy Davis. It was reported that the former president, at that point still alive but suffering from the advanced stages of Alzheimer's Disease, was not portrayed sympathetically. As one commentator put it after seeing advance clips from the show:

> Indeed, Brolin's heavily rouged, orange-haired Reagan is a caricature of the standard liberal caricature of Reagan. He is a doddering fool, stumbling around using his acting talents to pass for a statesman. His power-mad wife and a cabal of evil advisors make his decisions for him. His public affability and patriotism are just a façade over sanctimonious religious bigotry. When the film's Nancy Reagan advises him that the federal government should take steps to deal with AIDS, the film quotes him as saying, "They that live in sin shall die in sin." There is no source for such a quote, and the script-writer admits she invented the line, but this doesn't matter to the filmmakers. It serves their purpose, sliming Reagan.[46]

CBS was at pains to urge calm. When seen, network chairman Les Moonves insisted, the film would be judged a fair portrait of the former president and first lady. This was simply history, he suggested, with the good *and* the bad. "This was very important for me, to document everything and give a very fair point of view," Moonves said.[47] But then Judy Davis, costar of the mini-series, reacted to the mounting criticism with her own take on the state of freedom in America:

> With the climate that has been in America since Sept. 11, it appears, from the outside anyway, to not be quite as open a society as it used to be. By open, I mean as free in terms of a critical atmosphere, and that sort of ugly specter of patriotism. . . .
>
> If this film can help create a bit more questioning in the public about the direction America has been going in since the 1970's, I guess then I think it will be doing a service.[48]

Shortly thereafter, the *New York Times* reported, "CBS Is Said to Cancel Reagan Mini-Series." The story's lead ran thus:

> Under pressure from Republican and conservative groups, CBS is expected to announce as early as today that it is canceling its plans to run a two-part mini-series in November deconstructing the Ronald Reagan presidency, two people close to the decision said last night.[49]

But what mysterious power do the Republican Party and American conservatives hold over CBS? Is it not a smear to suggest that the pressure felt by CBS was from some, well, *vast right-wing conspiracy* rather than from nervous advertisers?

In the same issue of the *New York Times*, reporter Bernard Weinraub echoed the assertion that Mr. Reagan was suffering the effects of Alzheimer's while still in office: "In a recent interview Mr. Brolin [who plays RWR in *The Reagans*] said that the film depicted, to some degree, Mrs. Reagan taking control of the

White House as the president's health began to fail. Mr. Reagan has had Alzheimer's disease for years."[50] This clearly implies that Mr. Reagan was suffering the effects of Alzheimer's at some point prior to January 1989. Again, it is not possible dispositively to prove a negative. But the diagnosis of Alzheimer's was not made until November 1994, nearly six years after Reagan left office. Between 1989 and 1994 Reagan had made many public appearances, most notably his speech at the Republican convention in Houston in 1992. That speech had an autumnal quality to it, but there was no hint that the man delivering it did not know what he was saying.

The very next day after the initial reports that the mini-series might be canceled, the *Times* editorialized about CBS's decision to move *The Reagans* to its Showtime cable channel. The editorial wondered what CBS could possibly have been thinking: "[I]t should have come as no surprise that conservatives, protective of Mr. Reagan's image at all times, would launch one of the fierce assaults that have become so familiar whenever the right wants to scare the media on an ideological question."[51]

But why on earth would the mighty mainstream media be frightened of dissent, however "fiercely" expressed? And would the *Times* express the same alarm at a left-of-center movement that sought support from like-minded individuals for a boycott of a right-wing TV show? CBS, as I understand it, has had low ratings on other programs, and one wonders what damage would have been done to its reputation had the network stuck to its guns and aired the program it had supported enthusiastically until dissent was expressed—and a fewer than expected number of viewers had tuned in (exactly the consequence, by the way, of switching the program over to Showtime). And exactly what might have been the consequences to Moonves or any other executive at CBS of the "fierce assaults" to which the *Times* so ominously alluded? Bodily harm? Psychic wounds? I don't know Mr. Moonves, but I suspect he is a fairly hardy fellow and that he and his hard-charging colleagues, as true too of their friends at the *Times*, were unlikely to have suffered at all from any sort of "assault."

At this point Barbra Streisand weighed in with a rambling historical exegesis:

> I am deeply disappointed that CBS, the network that in 1964 gave me complete artistic control in creating television specials [*Color Me Barbra*], now caved in to right wing Republican pressure to cancel the network broadcast of the movie *The Reagans*. . . .
>
> Due to their experience with the restrictive English government, the framers of our Constitution specifically included a ban on prior restraint in the First Amendment [sic], which is an attempt to stop information from getting out there before the public has a chance to see it at all—exactly what is going on in this case. Of course, CBS as a company has the legal right to make decisions about what they do and do not air. However, these important decisions should be based on artistic integrity rather than an attempt to appease a small group of vocal dissidents. Indeed, today marks a sad day for artistic freedom—one of the most important elements of an open and democratic society.[52]

But if "today marks a sad day for artistic freedom," who is responsible for that result? The conservatives who freely expressed their opinions, or the network executives who backed out on their commitments?

The devaluation of Ronald Reagan is hardly limited to the liberal confines of TV. Despite the number of laudatory books published about the former president, the publishing industry itself remains skeptical of his achievements and of conservative historians who chronicle those achievements. As Paul Kengor points out—he is the author of two books about the late president— conservatives who write about Reagan can expect to see their work dismissed by *Publishers Weekly*, the "industry bible." What's curious about this, he notes, is the extent to which *PW*'s reviewers stand outside even the mainstream of liberal historical opinion about Reagan. "I'm not exaggerating," Prof. Kengor writes, "when I say that I could fill a book with encomiums on Reagan from left-leaning professors and journalists." [I must note here that two of his books about Mr. Reagan have been selections of American Compass, the book club of which I was editor in chief.] Kengor continues:

> If you are a conservative author who has written a favorable book on Ronald Reagan—no matter how insightful and well sourced—chances are extremely high that you will be zinged by *Publishers Weekly*, which will not merely be critical but will denigrate you and your work with the charge of "hagiography"—the scarlet H of biographical writing. This is a blistering criticism, done to signal to the wider industry to not take an author seriously. It is a term designed to ridicule and to discredit, to cause serious damage to not only a book but to the author's reputation. It should not be used lightly. And yet, *Publishers Weekly* applies the charge with abandon to conservative authors who dare to praise Reagan.[53]

In fact, "hagiography," which means, literally, a pious biography of a saint but also applies to any idealized story of any figure, is clearly intended as a smear. Kengor cites seven other serious books (besides his own) that were shunned by the influential trade magazine as "flattering," "admiring," "tender" "hagiography" (or, in one case, "hagiology").

Apparently no comparable word exists for books by liberals that attempt to discredit Reagan, unless that word would be "objective." As Kengor notes, *PW* extolled *Way Out There in the Blue: Reagan, Star Wars, and the End of the Cold War* (Simon & Schuster, 2000), by liberal *Nation* writer Frances FitzGerald, as "painstakingly detailed," and *PW* hailed liberal *Washington Post* writer Haynes Johnson's *Sleepwalking Through History* (W. W. Norton, 2003) as a "stunning indictment." One notes the titles of the two books and wonders at their objectivity, but *PW* cannot be bothered with acknowledging their bias—or the authors' liberalism—in its reviews. When it comes to conservatives, however, the political orientation of the author is always mentioned.

Conservatism as Pathology

It is one thing, we might say, to suggest that conservative, patriotic Americans are well organized and even constitute a kind of cabal when spurred to action, but quite another to assert that conservatism is actually a psychological pathology. Yet that's exactly what a group of researchers at the University of California, Berkeley, have done. In "Political Conservatism as Motivated Social Cognition," published in the American Psychological Association's *Psychological Bulletin*, the researchers have written that conservatism actually is a psychological disorder characterized by:

- Fear and aggression
- Dogmatism and intolerance of ambiguity

- Uncertainty avoidance
- Need for "cognitive closure"
- Terror management

To be sure, conservative radio personality and author Michael Savage (a longtime friend of the author of the book you are reading) wrote a book titled *Liberalism Is a Mental Disorder* (Nelson Current, 2005), but—rather as is the case with some of Ann Coulter's work—he was using a polemical metaphor.

That is not the case with the Berkeley study. As a university press release summarizes it:

> . . . [The researchers] sought patterns among 88 samples, involving 22,818 participants, taken from journal articles, books and conference papers. The material originating from 12 countries included speeches and interviews given by politicians, opinions and verdicts rendered by judges, as well as experimental, field and survey studies.
>
> Ten meta-analytic calculations performed on the material— which included various types of literature and approaches from different countries and groups—yielded consistent, common threads. . . . [54]

The results of this study of studies were stunning:

> Disparate conservatives share a resistance to change and acceptance of inequality, the authors said. Hitler, Mussolini, and former President Ronald Reagan were individuals, but all were right-wing conservatives because they preached a return to an idealized past and condoned inequality in some

form. Talk host Rush Limbaugh can be described the same way, the authors commented. . . . [55]

One might point out that the consequences of the years of the Reagan presidency were markedly different from those of Hitler's rule in Germany, but the researchers' point has been made, and the blow is little softened by their assurance that conservatism is not *necessarily* pathological even though, compared to liberals, conservatives are less "integratively complex."

Actually, this is nothing new. In the midst of the 1964 election campaign, *Fact* magazine published the results of a survey in which the same sort of elite opinion was expressed. *Time* magazine reported:

1,189 PSYCHIATRISTS SAY GOLDWATER IS PSY-CHOLOGICALLY UNFIT TO BE PRESIDENT! That determinedly flamboyant headline dressed the cover of *Fact* magazine one month before the presidential election of 1964. The entire issue was an examination of the "unconscious of a conservative," based largely on answers to a questionnaire sent to the 12,356 psychiatrists listed by the American Medical Association. Of the 2,417 who replied, 657 said Barry Goldwater was fit for the presidency, 571 declined to take a position, and 1,189 called him unfit—the latter in no uncertain terms. Some of their opinions: "emotionally unstable," "immature," "cowardly," "grossly psychotic," "paranoid," "mass murderer," "amoral and immoral," "chronic schizophrenic" and "dangerous lunatic." One psychiatrist even felt that a proposed Goldwater visit to Hitler's Berchtesgaden "is enough to convince me of his strong identification with the authoritarianism of Hitler, if not identification with Hitler himself."[56]

As Jonah Goldberg pointed out in an article about the Berkeley study, "So outrageous was this 'petition' of psychiatrists launched by *Fact* magazine that Goldwater actually won a libel suit, which is almost impossible for a politician."[57]

As for the Berkeley study, it seems clearly a smear undertaken behind the aura of science that uses some techniques of science but ignores others. What the researchers left out, first, was any clear definition of terms. They make much, for instance, about conservative "tolerance of inequality," which they treat as clearly retrograde, both socially and psychologically. What they fail to investigate is what is behind an acceptance of inequality. In some cases, it may be denigration of people different from oneself; in others, it may be a belief that individuals possess different abilities that naturally lead to disparate outcomes. From the conservative point of view, this is nothing more than an observation of fact. Indeed, while not suggesting that it represents any *psychological* disease, one might argue that the liberal insistence on equality is disordered with regard to the actual nature of things.

Second, the researchers accept a reading of history that is superficial at best. Yes, Hitler did cultivate a nostalgic vision of a Germanic past. But the name of his "Nazi" Party was a contraction of the German word *Nationalsozialismus*, meaning National Socialism. Any serious analysis of the Nazi program will discover that it had more in common with the communism of, say, the Soviet Union's Vladimir Lenin than with the conservatism of Reagan.

Finally, they simply ignore evidence that contradicts their conclusions. They lump Hitler in with Reagan (and, to be fair, one of the researchers later said he regretted that), but they fail to mention Lenin, Stalin, Mao, Pol Pot, or Fidel Castro, each of whom was (or in Castro's case *is*) famously aggressive, dogmatic, totalitarian, rigid, and violent. Yet nobody is likely to call Castro a conservative.

The best take on the Berkeley study came from Scott Ott at ScrappleFace, a conservative Web site devoted to comedic parody on news of the day. Ott "reported" on expressions of compassion from liberals:

> "Conservatives should not be debated, anymore than you would try to talk someone out of schizophrenia," said the lead researcher who wrote the journal article. "They are to be pitied, medicated and confined to institutions when necessary."
>
> Senate Minority Leader Tom Daschle said he was "deeply saddened" to hear of the plight of America's conservatives. He called on his colleagues to be "tolerant, patient, but never patronizing to those sick individuals on the other side of the aisle."
>
> While there is no cure for conservatism, early intervention by public schools and welfare agencies offers the best hope for prevention.[58]

As we'll see in this book's final chapter, *that* is the way to respond to a smear.

Patriotism as Pathology

Back in 1975, the English journalist Henry Fairlie wrote about American anti-Americanism: "The anti-American lives outside his country's present, in a myth of its past; and from this myth, he condemns what ought to be the numerous possibilities of its future to be those only of repetition, a curse that is never to be lifted."[59]

There is a reaction against imperfections in America that leads many in the elite—and those who follow elite opinion—to reject the American Dream simply because the dream is never completely realized. Once the dream is rejected, and with it the antecedents to the dream, there is no reason not to embrace other ideas, symbols, and dreams—often those that seem to contradict most strongly those of American tradition.

The same thing goes on in Europe and has for some time. Writing at about the same time as Fairlie, another English author, Peregrine Worsthorne, noted in *Encounter* magazine that:

> Europe accepts the idea that America is a country with a difference, from whom it is reasonable to demand an exceptionally altruistic standard of behavior. It feels perfectly justified in pouring obloquy on shortcomings from the ideal; and alas, perhaps inevitably, it seems to enjoy every example of a fall from grace which contemporary America provides.[60]

So it was and still is: so much is expected of America that America seems capable only of disappointing. Fairlie speculated that in Europe there is also a sense that America is still "too young," that it hasn't endured sufficient suffering to behave maturely. This sense, perhaps, explains the recent comment of the American expatriate actor Johnny Depp, who, in an interview with the German magazine *Stern*, said in reference to our involvement in Iraq:

America is dumb, it's like a dumb puppy that has big teeth that can bite and hurt you, aggressive. My daughter is four, my boy is one. I'd like them to see America as a toy, a broken toy. Investigate it a little, check it out, get this feeling and then get out.[61]

Shortly thereafter, Mr. Depp disavowed his comments, saying, in a statement issued by his publicist, that *Stern* had taken them out of context and that his criticisms of America simply reflect loving concern for his nation:

I am an American. I love my country and have great hopes for it. It is for this reason that I speak candidly and sometimes critically about it. I have benefited greatly from the freedom that exists in my country and for this I am eternally grateful.[62]

This seems to be a common theme: anti-Americanism *is* patriotism; dissent *is* the highest form of patriotism. But, whereas the willingness to take a stand against any injustice is completely laudable, the splenetic comments of Depp and others who despise America's imperfections hardly sound like expressions of love. "Relativism, and its twin Utopian perfectionism," writes Victor Davis Hanson, "make us uneasy with the idea of national unity and loyalty." He goes on:

These modern Sirens hypnotically whisper to us that since we cannot be 100 percent perfect, why even try? Who, after all, possesses enough morality, wisdom, or legitimate authority to promote "loyalty"—loyalty to what, to whom, when, where, and under what circumstances? We often quote Samuel Johnson's famous warning that "patriotism is the last refuge of a scoundrel"—but fail to note both that Johnson was talking specifically about false patriotism, and that elsewhere, on at least a half-dozen occasions, he praised both the patriot and the necessity of loyalty to one's country.[63]

But this is not the way the left sees it, is it? According to the Web site of CODEPINK, "a women-initiated grassroots peace and social justice movement,"

We cannot morally consent to war while paths of peace and negotiation have not been pursued to their fullest. We who cherish children will not consent to their murder. Nor do we consent to . . . the deaths of our own sons and daughters in a war for oil.

We love our country, but we will never wrap ourselves in red, white and blue. Instead, we announce a CODEPINK alert: signifying extreme danger to all the values of nurturing, caring, and compassion that women and loving men have held.[64]

One liberal Web site recently began merchandising what it calls a Progressive American Flag—Old Glory redesigned so the canton (the blue part) has, instead of stars, various symbols associated with the Left or the Green movement: the peace symbol, the two-finger salute weirdly appropriated by the antiwar movement from Winston Churchill, the Yin-Yang, an equals sign, a heart, a recycling emblem, and a bicycle. In the red stripes in the flag's field are, as the designer explains, "a collage of photographs I took of the protest of the Republican National Convention on August 29, 2004," and in the white stripes are the following quotations:

Dissent is the highest form of patriotism.

—HOWARD ZINN

The only way to make sure people you agree with can speak is to support the rights of people you don't agree with.

—ELEANOR HOLMES NORTON

It is the first responsibility of every citizen to question authority.

—BENJAMIN FRANKLIN

No matter that patriotism is too often the refuge of scoundrels. Dissent, rebellion and all-around hell-raising remain the true duty of patriots.

—BARBARA EHRENREICH

We must not confuse dissent with disloyalty. When the loyal opposition dies, I think the soul of America dies with it.

—EDWARD R. MURROW

Moral cowardice that keeps us from speaking our minds is as dangerous to this country as irresponsible talk. The right way is not always the popular and easy way. Standing for right when it is unpopular is a true test of moral character.

—MARGARET CHASE SMITH

"Display this flag," the designer writes, "and you'll not only be showing your own true colors, you'll be preserving a piece of history lost in the hysterical Fox News accounts of violent rioting in New York City."

I can only assume the "violent rioting" to which he refers are the various protests outside the 2004 Republican National Convention. Typical was the protest outside the convention site of the advocacy group ACT UP (AIDS Coalition to Unleash Power), a "naked protest" intended to "tell 'the naked truth' about Bush's global AIDS policies."[65] As with nearly all the arrests made at the convention (90 percent), the arrested naked protesters were later released. As for the violence arising from the protests, it was mostly instigated by protestors against the police.

The police, in this case the legendary NYPD, were actually well prepared for the protests, having done surveillance on many of the radical groups that had made clear their intention to disrupt Republican convention activities. After it was revealed that the police had done such surveillance, the *New York Times* railed on its front page against the cops for their "aggressive" intelligence-gathering. But as a *New York Post* editorial pointed out, after its Page One attack on the police the *Times* itself admitted on an inside page that the NYPD had been granted "greater authority from a federal judge to investigate political organizations for criminal activity."[66] The *Post* editorial, "Smearing the NYPD," wondered: "What were the police supposed to do? Wait for the riots to start, à la Seattle [where antiglobalist demonstrators had disrupted a 1999 meeting of the World Trade Organization]? For the bombs to go off, à la Madrid [where al Qaeda bombed railways in 2004]?"

Patriots Smearing Patriots?

Alas, smears aren't confined to the Left. No political smear in recent memory had as much press play—or has been as much disputed—as an attack on Sen. John McCain during the 2000 presidential primary in South Carolina. Long story short: Sen. McCain had upset George W. Bush in the New Hampshire primary and rolled into South Carolina with a chance to seriously, perhaps permanently, damage Gov. Bush's chances for the GOP nomination. However, during the Palmetto State campaign someone did what is known as a "push poll," in which polemical and leading questions are part of an ostensible opinion survey. This one *allegedly* included the question: "Would you be more likely or less likely to vote for John McCain for president if you knew he had fathered an illegitimate black child?"[67]

This is akin to the classic lawyer smear-question, *Exactly when, sir, did you stop beating your wife?*, when no previous allegation of wife-beating is on the record.

Problem is, no one has ever produced any evidence that the question about an illegitimate black child was actually included in any Bush-campaign telephone polling. Records from the company hired to do "advocacy" calls to South Carolinians reveal no such question. Audio tapes exist of negative push polling by both the Bush and the McCain campaigns, especially during the later Michigan primary, but none of these contain the illegitimate-black-child smear.[68] Understand: 200,000 calls were made in South Carolina, yet nobody ended up with a sample of the smear on an answering machine.

There is no doubt that the smear was bruited about during the primary campaign. As Richard Davis wrote in the March 21,

2004, edition of *The Boston Globe*, It appears to have had its origin in an e-mail sent by a professor from Bob Jones University, Richard Hand, to "fellow South Carolinians" stating that McCain had "chosen to sire children without marriage." Behind the smear was the fact that McCain and his wife, Cindy, are the adoptive parents of a dark-skinned girl, Bridget, whom they found in a Bangladeshi orphanage run by the Sisters of Charity, the order founded by Mother Teresa of Calcutta.

But the lack of any evidence connecting the smear to the Bush campaign has not stopped anti-Bush partisans (Democrats and Republicans) from charging that the smear question was in those polls and was the work of the Bush team's chief strategist, Karl Rove. James Moore and Wayne Slater, the authors of the 2004 book *Bush's Brain* [Wiley, 2003] (subsequently made into a documentary film), repeat the smear and further assert that Karl Rove engineered it. And so the original smear against Sen. McCain, whatever its shape, has been hijacked to smear Rove and Bush.

The use of smears in campaigns is common enough, as we saw again in the 2006 Senate contest in Virginia between Republican incumbent George Allen and Democratic challenger—and eventual winner—James Webb, a novelist and former Reagan administration aide. As CNN reported:

> In a news release and list of quotes posted . . . on the Drudge Report Web site, Sen. George Allen accused his opponent, former Navy Secretary Jim Webb, of "demeaning women" and "dehumanizing women, men and even children" through his fiction writings. At least two of the listed passages include children in sexual situations.[69]

Webb was understandably upset, though he was unable to resist a smear of his own: "This is a Karl Rove campaign," he said. Rove was not involved in Sen. Allen's campaign.

Meanwhile, Sen. Allen's selective citation of lurid passages from Webb's novels was too much even for the conservative *Washington Times*. Writing on the *Times* Web site, blogger Scott Galupo called Sen. Allen an "opportunistic philistine" and compared the allegations made against Webb's writing to the attacks on Vladimir Nabokov after the publication of *Lolita*.

> Some readers refused to accept that someone who wrote in a fictional context about pedophilia did not approve of pedophilia—or, worse, was a pedophile himself.
>
> If, today, anyone is scandalized by what Webb wrote, that's their right—and their folly.[70]

Sen. Allen also pointed out that, in a 1979 magazine article, Webb had questioned the role of women in combat and referred to his alma mater, the United States Naval Academy, as a "horny woman's dream." Webb apologized.

Webb's campaign then prepared an attack ad alleging that Sen. Allen had failed to properly declare profits from some stock options—a charge that a Senate committee subsequently ruled was baseless. Author and activist Cal Thomas, himself a Virginia resident, wrote:

> One must conclude that, since the information was available to Webb and [Democratic Senatorial Campaign Committee head Sen. Chuck] Schumer, the two deliberately used factual inaccuracies in the negative ad. But why let truth get in the

way of an effective election strategy? The damage was done and since the ad fit nicely into the Democrats' theme of "the culture of corruption" in the Republican majority, the desired result was achieved. Allen lost the election by 9,000 votes.[71]

Thomas concludes: "Allen made his share of mistakes during his re-election campaign, but this was not one of them. His opponent and Sen. Schumer, neither of whom has apologized or retracted their accusations, unfairly smeared him."

Looking at the Allen-Webb race, former Virginia governor Mark Warner, a Democrat, characterized the Allen campaign's tactics this way: "All they do is smear, smear, smear."[72] He might have said the same about the other side. In any case, in a campaign such as this it's hard to say that the voters come away particularly satisfied when two fundamentally decent men, patriots both, engage in smear tactics.

III

SMEARING SOLDIERS

We the people, especially the moms, of America need to wake up and realize that wars are seldom fought to preserve our freedom and democracy, but rather to make rich people richer and powerful people even more powerful. We need to stop allowing the war machine to eat our children and spit out money.

—Antiwar activist Cindy Sheehan[1]

THERE'S ANOTHER TERM THAT MAY STAND in the place of the word *smear*: "defamatory innuendo." It's one used in a February 2005 *Wall Street Journal* article by Bret Stephens to summarize what he'd recently heard Eason Jordan, then chief news executive of the Cable News Network (CNN), say at the World Economic Forum in Davos, Switzerland:

Mr. Jordan observed that of the 60-odd journalists killed in Iraq, 12 had been targeted and killed by coalition forces. . . .
    Here Rep. Barney Frank [D-MA] . . . interjected: Had American troops actually targeted journalists? And had CNN done a story about it? Well no, Mr. Jordan replied. . . . And no, he didn't believe the Bush administration had a

policy of targeting journalists. Besides, he said, "the [American] generals and colonels have their heart in the right place."

By this point, one could almost see the wheels of Mr. Jordan's mind spinning, slowly: "How am I going to get out of this one?"

Stephens, a member of the *Journal*'s editorial board, concluded that whether or not Jordan had intended to, he'd made a defamatory innuendo, which "rather than outright allegation—is the vehicle of mainstream media bias."[2] Eason Jordan resigned from CNN the next day.

Stephens's eyewitness account was quickly joined by several others—which was the outside world's only source of information, as officials at the World Economic Forum refused to release a recording of Jordan's remarks. The *Washington Post*'s Howard Kurtz talked to David Gergen, who was the moderator of that panel:

> David Gergen, editor at large at *U.S. News & World Report*, said he "sort of gasped" when Jordan spoke of journalists being "deliberately killed," but that Jordan "realized, as soon as he said it, he'd gone too far" and "walked it back." Jordan then expressed "a very deep concern about whether our soldiers on the ground level are using as much care as they should" when journalists are involved, said Gergen.[3]

Author and blogger Michelle Malkin pointed out in the *New York Post* that this wasn't the first time Jordan had been involved in a smear of American soldiers:

Jordan's the man who admitted last spring that CNN withheld news out of Baghdad to maintain access to Saddam
Hussein's regime. He was quoted last fall telling a Portu-
guese forum that he believed journalists had been arrested
and tortured by American forces (a charge he maintains
today). . . . He was in the middle of the infamous Tailwind
scandal, in which CNN was forced to retract a Peter Arnett
report that the American military used sarin gas against
its own troops in Laos. And in 1999, Jordan declared: "We
are a global network, and we take global interest[s] first, not
U.S. interests first."

Now, who is more deserving of the benefit of the doubt?
Eason Jordan or our men and women on the battlefield? I
support the troops.[4]

It's a fair question, and one that evokes a long history—at least
since the Vietnam War—of media hostility to the armed forces.
Indeed, the Left is at war with the military, and it's the one war
they must not win. Destroy faith, demean patriotism, eviscerate
conservatism, wreck capitalism, and still a semblance of America
will endure—probably to rise up and correct the errors. But succeed in making us all into pacifists and in disarming our soldiers,
sailors, airmen, and Marines, and we will be lost without hope of
recovery.

"Fake But Accurate"

One of the most egregious smears in recent memory was CBS's
smear of George W. Bush's service record in the Air National
Guard. It perfectly captures the sense of leftist desperation about

the failure of the democratic process to achieve the Mandarins' ends.

In May 1968, Mr. Bush signed up for a six-year term as a pilot in the Guard. Over the next four years he accumulated far more than the fifty "points" required to fulfill his obligation. However, in May 1972, he requested transfer from his Texas unit to the 187th Tactical Reconnaissance Group of the Alabama Air National Guard, since he wanted to work on the campaign of a senatorial candidate there. Records from the future president's time in Alabama are sparse, and some people have accused him of being absent without leave (AWOL) during part of his service there. The Democrats took up this theme early in the 2004 presidential campaign, and in February 2004 NBC's Tim Russert raised the question during an interview, prompting the White House to release the president's service records. *National Review*'s Byron York summarized these:

> In his first four years of service, Bush piled up lots of points; he earned 253 points in his first year, 340 in his second, 137 in his third, and 112 in his fourth. For the year from May 1972 to May 1973, records show Bush earned 56 points, a much smaller total, but more than the minimum requirement (his service was measured on a May-to-May basis because he first joined the Guard in that month in 1968).
>
> Bush then racked up another 56 points in June and July of 1973, which met the minimum requirement for the 1973–74 year, which was Bush's last year of service. Together, the record "clearly shows that First Lieutenant George W. Bush has satisfactory years for both '72–'73 and '73–'74, which proves that he completed his military obligation in a satisfactory manner," says retired Lt. Col. Albert Lloyd, a Guard

personnel officer who reviewed the records at the request of the White House.[5]

So it was a sensational moment when, during a September 8, 2004, broadcast of *60 Minutes Wednesday*, correspondent Dan Rather presented a series of documents dated from May 4, 1972, to August 18, 1973, supposedly from the "personal files" of Lt. Bush's commanding officer, Lt. Col. Jerry B. Killian. The first of the documents was apparently signed by Killian; the others were unsigned. Rather said that the documents had been authenticated by the network's experts. They started out with a notice to Lt. Bush advising him that he is due for his annual physical, and concluded with a "Memo to File" indicating that Lt. Bush had disobeyed orders and then used political muscle to cover up his offenses. The final memo read:

Memo to File
SUBJECT: CYA

1. Staudt has obviously pressured Hodges more about Bush. I'm having trouble running interference and doing my job. Harris gave me a message today from Grp regarding Bush's OETR and Staudt is pushing to sugar coat it. Bush wasn't here during rating period and I don't have any feedback from 187th in Alabama. I will not rate. Austin is not happy today either.
2. Harris took the call from Grp today. I'll backdate but won't rate. Harris agrees.[6]

As it happens, the experts to whom Rather referred had not been in agreement about the authenticity of the memos. In fact, as *The*

Washington Post reported on September 15, 2004, after comparing the documents in question to others with Colonel Killian's signature, none was willing to say for certain that the memos were authentic. Two of the four experts consulted had qualms about the typeface employed in the memos and suggested that *60 Minutes* producer Mary Mapes consult a forensic typewriter expert. But when the expert reached CBS—still prior to the broadcast—he was told that his services were not needed.

That was unfortunate, since within hours after the CBS segment, titled "For the Record," was aired, it became clear that the Killian memos were forgeries. There were many reasons that this became clear—and the Power Line blog led the way in exposing them—but sufficient for our purpose is one simple fact: the name of the Guard unit was presented in the memo as "187th," which is to say with a superscript "th."[7] In all other Killian documents the unit was typed as the "187th." (In those pre-personal-computer days, it would have required a special effort to type a superscript character on a typewriter.) But there were more substantive errors in the memo as well. As John Hinderaker of the Power Line blog wrote:

> The most important such error was the anachronistic effort to portray Brig. Gen. "Buck" Staudt as pressuring Lt. Col. Bobby Hodges to "sugar coat" Lt. Bush's evaluation—a year and a half after Staudt retired from the Texas Air National Guard. This was the most important of the CBS documents, and based on its content alone, it was an obvious fraud, both fake and inaccurate. Case closed.[8]

Despite the evidence against authenticity that surfaced so quickly, CBS stuck to its guns, claiming its source for the memos was "unimpeachable." However, when that source—not initially identified by CBS—turned out to be one retired Lt. Col. Bill Burkett, who has been described in mild terms as a "longtime Bush critic," it was clear that another serpent had been loosed on an American president.

When concerns about the validity of the Killian memos were raised, Burkett said first that he had received the documents from George Conn—like Burkett, a former member of the Texas National Guard. Then he said he had received them from one Lucy Ramirez, whose identity has never been established. He first asserted that the documents were authentic, and then that he had doubts about their authenticity. He also said that to protect Ms. Ramirez, he burned the original papers (after making copies at Kinko's) in order to destroy any DNA that might link her to the story.[9]

Indeed, Bill Burkett seems to be a latter-day James Callender. He even turned on CBS, threatening to sue the network for damaging his reputation by failing to determine that the memos he submitted were forgeries.[10] (It may be necessary to read that last sentence more than once.) Ed Driscoll of the Captain's Quarters blog suggested that Burkett had "all the earmarks of a pathological liar":

> For those of us who have personal experience with this type of person, these signs look appallingly familiar. Burkett starts with a lie . . . that gets debunked. He tries to back his lie up with an escalating series of lies, culminating in the forgeries. He passes them off to CBS and *USA Today* by claiming a source that's conveniently overseas. When those blow up in his face (in small part because the forgeries use Army lingo, Burkett's branch, instead of Air Force), he then spins tales of

a mysterious woman who sends an intermediary to deliver envelopes full of documents but who later insists that he burn the evidence. Her name is conveniently common enough in Texas to thwart any effective checking of her identity, and now he claims to be a "patsy." When challenged, he reacts by . . . making melodramatic statements.[11]

This may explain why Burkett did what he did. But why did CBS join the charade? Why did a CBS producer reach out to this opponent of President Bush to obtain this story? And why did that same CBS producer put Burkett in touch with John Kerry's presidential campaign team, saying to Kerry adviser Joe Lockhart that Burkett had some records "that might move the story forward"?[12] The answer is fairly obvious to me: to smear George W. Bush.

Whether or not Burkett created the fake documents, and whether or not CBS believed at any point that they were real, it became clear that, as Dan Rather later said, it was no longer possible to have the "confidence in these documents that would allow us to continue vouching for them journalistically."[13] Yet Mary Mapes would later echo, in her book *Truth and Duty*, the claim made by Col. Killian's eighty-six-year-old former secretary, Marian Carr Knox, that the Killian memos were "fake but accurate." Mapes wrote:

There was no analysis [by critics] of what the documents actually said, no work done to look at the content, no comparison with the official record, no phone calls made to check the facts of the story, nothing beyond a cursory and politically motivated examination of the typeface. That was all they had to attack, but that was enough.[14]

As blogger Rand Simberg wrote of Miss Mapes's claim, "My irony meter just shattered the glass, and bent its needle into a pretzel."[15]

It seems hardly necessary to say out loud, but a faked document can make no claim to accuracy. Writing at the Independent Women's Forum Web site, Charlotte Allen summed the case up perfectly:

> Fake but accurate—Mary Mapes admits that was a good enough standard for her. And nowadays it's a good enough standard for many a journalist and scholar, as long as they've got the proper crusading credentials. In other words, it's OK to make things up in the service of a Greater Truth.[16]

Both Dan Rather and Mary Mapes lost their jobs at CBS over the controversy, but this is a rare case in which a contemporary smear campaign has redounded to the detriment of the smear merchant. The emerging blogosphere may make such cases less rare, since bloggers are a diverse group with wide-ranging expertise and can quickly expose the kind of shenanigans CBS employed. But twenty-five years ago no harm came to the perpetrators of one of the most spectacular of all journalistic smears—also, as it happens, on CBS.

Smearing Westmoreland

In January 1982, *CBS Reports* aired a documentary, *The Uncounted Enemy: A Vietnam Deception*, by reporter Mike Wallace and producer George Crile. In it, Wallace baited Gen. William Westmoreland with belligerent questions based upon evidence provided by a source the network had reason to suspect was not unbiased, former CIA consultant Sam Adams. The gist of the CBS charge was that back in 1967–68 Gen. Westmoreland, commander of American forces in Vietnam, and his staff at the Military Assistance Command Vietnam (MACV) deliberately suppressed intelligence and understated North Vietnamese troop strength in order to keep President Johnson, Congress, and the American people from learning how perilous the situation was.[17] Mike Wallace led off the show by saying, "Tonight we're going to present evidence of what we have come to believe was a conscious effort—indeed a conspiracy at the highest levels of American intelligence—to suppress and alter critical intelligence on the enemy leading up to the Tet offensive [in January 1968]. . . ."[18]

The show aired Saturday, January 23. The following Tuesday, General Westmoreland called a press conference at Washington's Army-Navy Club at which he and several of his MACV colleagues refuted CBS's charges point by point. General Westmoreland demanded a retraction; CBS refused; the General sued George Crile, Mike Wallace, and the network for libel.

Meanwhile, two authors for *TV Guide*, not normally known for engaging in investigative journalism, painstakingly sifted the evidence and found that CBS had specifically excluded from the documentary witnesses who contradicted the network's thesis. "Anatomy of a Smear: How CBS News Broke the Rules and 'Got' Gen. Westmoreland"[19] was a devastating blow to CBS, demonstrating that the reporter and the producer had ridden roughshod over "commonly accepted rules of their business" and trashed their own internal guidelines.[20] A later internal report at CBS, known as the Benjamin Report, corroborated the *TV Guide* account. For instance, the report quotes Gen. Phillip Davidson:

During the Vietnam War the dissemination of certain very sensitive intelligence was limited to a few civilian and military leaders in key positions. This was necessary to protect the source of the intelligence. . . . Most of the junior officers who appeared on the program had no access to this sensitive intelligence. Their superiors, who did have access, often disapproved the work of the junior analysts because the senior official knew . . . that the analyst's views were invalid, inaccurate, or incomplete.[21]

Two years later—once the lawsuit had reached the courtroom— the network issued a weak apology, saying it never intended to impugn the general's patriotism, and he dropped his suit. CBS subsequently lost its libel insurance, but most Americans who remember the controversy probably still believe that Westmoreland was guilty as charged.

Code Red at CODEPINK

The smearing of the American military goes on. So far, however, America's armed forces continue to thrive. One of the more startling (and satisfying) facts of the last few years is that in the 2006 graduating class of the United States Naval Academy more midshipmen declared for the marine corps than at any other point in Academy history. In the army, although enlistment goals have recently been a struggle to achieve, *re-enlistment* rates are higher than ever. And, despite the negative tenor of reporting on the wars in Afghanistan and Iraq and the brutal nature of those conflicts, morale is high throughout the services. (It should also be noted that it's only the army that has experienced a recruiting shortfall. The other branches—Marines, navy, and air force—have all recently exceeded their goals.) And, in opinion polls, the military ranks high on lists of the most admired institutions. According to a recent Gallup poll, the military actually tops the list of institutions eliciting a "great deal" or "quite a lot" of confidence: 74 percent for the armed forces, 63 percent for the police, 53 percent for organized religion.[22] But this admiration isn't shared by the Left.

In the introduction to *10 Excellent Reasons Not to Join the Military*, from which the epigraph for this chapter is taken, antiwar activist Cindy Sheehan provides an answer to what might replace a strong American military: "We need to demand that our leaders use their words to solve problems. We need to demand that other nations use their words, too."

"[U]se their words" is the kind of thing heard from the lips of mothers attempting to quiet a little girl's tantrum or correct the behavior of a boy who expresses anger with his fists: *Use your words, Billy. It's not nice to hit.* This is the *Sesame Street* approach to international relations. It may work as a technique of motherly discipline, but it is hopelessly naïve as an approach to foreign policy. It is a fantasy of the kind that George Bernard Shaw was thinking of when he wrote: "Hell is paved with good intentions, not with bad ones. All men mean well." And women, too.

Antiwar activists such as Sheehan often insist that they support American troops and oppose only the misguided policies of the American government. This may be true of some. It is not true of others, such as the members of CODEPINK, mentioned in Chapter 2. CODEPINK is a self-identified group of "rabble-rousers" that regularly protests outside of army hospitals, such as Walter Reed in Bethesda, Maryland. CODEPINK offers what it calls counter-recruitment posters ("You Can't Be All That You

Can Be if You're Dead") and various antimilitary publications, including the aforementioned *10 Excellent Reasons Not to Join the
Military*. In one of that volume's essays, Rae Abileah—a coordi-
nator for CODEPINK—writes about her decision not to join the
military. She had considered doing so while still in high school,
she tells us, on the assumption that her service would earn her
money for college under the G.I. Bill. Ultimately she took another route. She explains:

> I did not join the Army because I realized that I had choices
> and that joining the military was not the only way to go to
> college or become a strong woman. And at that time, I didn't
> even know that, according to the Central Committee for
> Conscientious Objectors, 60 percent of all recruits never re-
> ceive any money for college.[23]

This may be what the Central Committee for Conscientious Ob-
jectors maintains, but the Department of Veterans Affairs tells a
rather different story: in fiscal 2005, the G.I. Bill "usage rate" for
participating veterans was 71 percent.[24] Of course, there are some
members of the armed forces who choose not to participate in
the program. This is a distressing matter for the Department of
Veterans Affairs, but it is *not* what Abileah is asserting.

The sense of Abileah's essay is that the armed forces dupe into
the military young people not savvy enough to attend college or
do alternative kinds of service to the nation:

> There is a great sense of pride in American culture about serv-
> ing our country through the armed services—or at least there's
> a lot of media hype and seductive advertising about it. Though
> not as visibly glamorous, it takes more honor and courage to

dedicate one's life to working for social change. Teachers, community organizers, activists, engineers, public defense attorneys, lobbyists, and artists are the true patriots. . . . [25]

She does not explain why, putting aside the matter of honor, more courage is required to work for social change in America than to face terrorists in Afghanistan or Iraq.

Having suggested that most recruits sign up because they have been duped, Abileah then goes on to offer an even more patronizing reason that some young people join the armed forces: they lead such low-rent lives that the military is actually a step up:

> Young folks who grow up in low-income areas or troubled households might be attracted to the discipline and strength promised by the military, as a direct contrast to the disorder and loss of control they feel at home. Additionally, the institutionalized violence that the military represents seems to provide a socially acceptable use of street survival skills that might otherwise land a person in jail. When a young person is failing out of school, taking drugs, or experiencing family violence at home, he or she likely feels weak. "The offer of physical prowess and the power commanded by wearing the Army uniform can become very enticing, beyond the financial incentives offered by the military," suggests Galen Petersen, musician and co-founder of Art in Action, an arts and activism summer camp for underprivileged youth.

Not content with smearing the young people who choose the military, Abileah goes on to smear the Armed Forces themselves. Her essay concludes:

Maybe a sentence or two of this writing will fertilize a blossoming mind and sprout the idea that when there is no way out, it is not the time to give in to this child-killing machine called the military; it's time to resist.

The assumptions represented in this CODEPINK publication may seem to be way out on the fringes of liberal thinking, but this appears not to be the case. Consider the recent statements of Sen. John Kerry of Massachusetts and Rep. Charles Rangel of New York, both of whom have suggested that military service is for those not smart enough to avoid it. The repetition of such a claim is certainly a smear.

Study Hard

It was back in April 1971 that future U.S. senator and presidential candidate John Kerry testified before the United States Senate that American servicemen in Vietnam had

> . . . raped, cut off ears, cut off heads, taped wires from portable telephones to human genitals and turned up the power, cut off limbs, blown up bodies, randomly shot at civilians, razed villages in fashion reminiscent of Genghis Khan, shot cattle and dogs for fun, poisoned food stocks, and generally ravaged the countryside of South Vietnam in addition to the normal ravage of war, and the normal and very particular ravaging which is done by the applied bombing power of this country.[26]

Later in his testimony, Mr. Kerry said:

We rationalized destroying villages in order to save them. We saw America lose her sense of morality as she accepted very coolly a My Lai and refused to give up the image of American soldiers who hand out chocolate bars and chewing gum.

To be sure, there were atrocities committed by Americans against the people of Vietnam, as there are lapses of civilized behavior in every war. The My Lai Massacre in 1968, in which a detachment of men from the army's Americal division indiscriminately killed as many as five hundred villagers, is an egregious example. But Mr. Kerry's characterization is a smear of the overwhelming majority of soldiers and Marines who served honorably and who observed the rule of law and, beyond the simple distribution of Hershey bars and Wrigley's spearmint, gave their hearts, souls, and lives to win the freedom of the Vietnamese people.

The source for Mr. Kerry's charges was the Winter Soldier Investigation, which had been carried out by Kerry's organization, Vietnam Veterans Against the War, several months before his Senate testimony. Trouble is, as Mackubin Thomas Owens has written, the investigation was hampered by fraudulent testimony.

It was inspired by Mark Lane's 1970 book entitled *Conversations with Americans*, which claimed to recount atrocity stories by Vietnam veterans. This book was panned by James Reston Jr. and Neil Sheehan, not exactly known as supporters of the Vietnam War. Sheehan in particular demonstrated that many of Lane's "eye witnesses" either had never served in Vietnam or had not done so in the capacity they claimed.[27]

As William Tecumseh Sherman famously observed, "War is hell," and all men—including American soldiers—are subject to temptation to the kind of sinful behavior represented by the My Lai Massacre. However, what is not often remembered about My Lai is that in the midst of this outrage an American helicopter gunship landed between the Vietnamese and the Americal platoon led by Lt. William Calley. The chopper's pilot, Warrant Officer Hugh Thompson Jr., warned the American soldiers that he would open fire on them if the massacre continued.[28]

Lt. Calley was convicted in a court-martial in March 1971 and sentenced to life in prison, though in the end he served just three and a half years. It is not the purpose of this book to consider the reasons—legal and political—for Calley's light prison term, but it is important to recall that he was sentenced, and also that the national uproar when the details of My Lai came out can hardly be characterized as America accepting it "very coolly."

As Owens also writes, "While left-wing anti-war critics of U.S. policy in Vietnam were always quick to invoke Auschwitz and the Nazis in discussing alleged American atrocities, they were silent about Hué City, where a month and a half before My Lai, the North Vietnamese and VC systematically murdered 3,000 people."[29] And by "systematically" he means *as a matter of policy*. But more temperate observers than Mark Lane or the young John Kerry see American actions at My Lai for what they were: a set of criminal acts that had nothing to do with our policy. Most American soldiers obey the rules of war, and when they don't they are held accountable. Meanwhile the Left is silent—then as now—on the way America's enemies make murder the rule.

It is instructive, as Brent Bozell of the Media Research Center points out, that during the 2004 presidential campaign, very few national media made reference to Mr. Kerry's 1971 Senate testimony:

> How many times have our most "reliable" hard news outlets passed along this passage of monstrous American evil that so inflames the veterans against John Kerry? A Nexis search reveals a list of some of the national outlets that had *never* relayed a quote of these words before the second Swift Vet ad was released: CBS, NBC, National Public Radio, *Time*, *Newsweek*, *U.S. News & World Report*, the *Los Angeles Times*, and *USA Today*. Here are the major newspapers who've captured this testimony exactly *once*: *The Washington Post* and *The New York Times*, buried inside their papers on Saturdays in late February. ABC repeated one snippet of the paragraph, the "Genghis Khan" snippet, in four stories surrounding the anniversary of the testimony in April [2004]. Kerry said then: "I'm sorry that they're offended by that, but that's what happened."[30]

Mr. Kerry had established a meme that is regularly applied in the press to the current war in Iraq. In a July 2, 2006, article in the *Gainesville Sun*, Vietnam veteran Chas Chiodo wrote that although many people say they oppose the Iraq war but support the American troops fighting it, he does not.

> Although little Johnny or Judy might have once been that nice kid next door, he or she may now be engaged in massacres and atrocities. "The troops" are waging war against a civilian population, making little or no attempt to distinguish between "insurgents" and "collateral" innocents in the

vicinity. When faced with frequent sniping, mines, ambushes and treachery by supposed local "allies," even the best-trained occupation armies soon become brutal, sadistic, cynical and demoralized. Torture and atrocities happen in all wars, on both sides. None are right, but America has to accept the fact that when little Johnny or Judy enlists in one of the branches of service, he becomes a hired killer.[31]

When he served in Vietnam, Chiodo says, the military "was composed of many different kinds of people, including a fair share of losers, brutes and bloodthirsty thugs," and he believes nothing has changed.

I believe that every one of the U.S. government's military and "civil" agents in Iraq are engaged in "a war of unprovoked aggression," and therefore all bear some guilt for participating in an evil enterprise. I am not suggesting that the man who drives a supply truck is as guilty as the man who shoots a baby at point blank range, but all of our forces are guilty to some degree. Doing wrong is doing wrong, be it in Gainesville or Iraq. Bush told the soldiers to go, and they chose to obey. When the Nazis at Nuremberg claimed they were "only following orders," they received no mercy, nor did they deserve any. Perhaps the enlisted men and women who merely tagged along are less culpable than Bush, but nobody involved in this huge criminal undertaking is entitled to a clean bill of moral health.

Chiodo's was a sentiment similar to that expressed by *Los Angeles Times* columnist Joel Stein, whose January 24, 2006, column,

"Warriors and Wusses," begins with the line: "I don't support the troops." And his reasons are pretty much the same as Chiodo's:

> The truth is that people who pull triggers are ultimately responsible, whether they're following orders or not. An army of people making individual moral choices may be inefficient, but an army of people ignoring their morality is horrifying. . . .
>
> [W]hen you volunteer for the U.S. military, you pretty much know you're not going to be fending off invasions from Mexico and Canada. So you're willingly signing up to be a fighting tool of American imperialism, for better or worse. Sometimes you get lucky and get to fight ethnic genocide in Kosovo, but other times it's Vietnam.[32]

For his part, John Kerry famously voted for Iraq war appropriations . . . before he voted against them. Both the initial vote and the flip-flop haunted him throughout the 2004 presidential campaign. Another thing that haunted him was the sudden surfacing of some of his Vietnam-era comrades in arms.

Although *Publishers Weekly* named as 2004's Book of the Year *America (The Book)* by comedian Jon Stewart and his staff at *The Daily Show*, the most significant book published during that heated political year was surely *Unfit for Command: Swift Boat Veterans Speak Out Against John Kerry* (Regnery Publishing, 2004) by John O'Neill and Jerome Corsi. It's fair to say, I think, that the "Swift Boat" book was a specter hanging over the Kerry campaign from its publication in August until the November voting. To many Kerry supporters, *Unfit for Command* was a smear, plain and simple.

Despite his Winter Soldier assertions and his prominence in that forum, John Kerry's military record is stellar: three Purple Hearts for combat wounds received and Bronze and Silver Stars for valor—all awarded as a consequence of just four months of service in Vietnam in 1968–69. For some reason, however, the senator has yet to authorize the release of the full record of his service, and because of that—and because he made his service the centerpiece of his presidential campaign—legitimate questions remain about his record. Do those questions outweigh Mr. Kerry's medals? The Swift Boat Veterans for Truth believed they do, which led to their indictment of the Kerry record. The *Washington Post* editorialized that the Swifties' criticisms ("branding Mr. Kerry a coward and a liar") were a smear. Indeed, one of the veterans involved, George Elliott, Mr. Kerry's former commanding officer, was the very man who had recommended the future senator for the medals he received, and objections raised about the Purple Hearts were certainly a stretch, since Mr. Kerry never asserted that his shrapnel wounds were anything but minor and since the seriousness of a wound received in combat isn't among the criteria for awarding the medal. And of his heroism in rescuing a fallen comrade, the contradictory testimony of several members of Swift Boat Veterans for Truth can hardly trump the firsthand statement of the man he rescued, Jim Rassmann, who says the Swifties were wrong. And he should know.[33]

Not that members of the press made the slightest effort to actually investigate the claims made in *Unfit for Command* or in Swift Boat Veterans for Truth ads or in appearances various Swifties made on TV and radio talk shows. In the summer of 2004, the Media Research Center found that whereas the three major networks (ABC, CBS, and NBC) had run seventy-five stories so far that year questioning the National Guard service of President Bush, they'd done just nine on the Swift Boat controversy.[34]

And many of those stories—and the Kerry campaign—blamed Mr. Bush for the Swift Boat attacks, despite the fact that neither the president's campaign staff nor the Republican National Committee either endorsed or supported the Swifties in any way. Quite the opposite, in fact. As Mort Kondracke wrote—admittedly before the publication of *Unfit for Command*—"the Bush campaign and the GOP have acknowledged time and again that Kerry was a war hero and is due honor for his service. . . ." It was his record on defense appropriations and foreign-policy issues that the GOP came at hard. When GOP chairman Edward Gillespie listed the weapons system against which Sen. Kerry had voted, the Senator's campaign claimed Gillespie was making "another desperate attack on the patriotism of John Kerry."[35]

But Mr. Kerry's military problems didn't end with his concession speech on November 3, 2004. Speaking before a group of students in California in October 2006, Mr. Kerry seemed to smear soldiers yet again: "You know, education, if you make the most of it, you study hard, and you do your homework, and you make an effort to be smart, you can do well. If you don't, you get stuck in Iraq."

Reaction to the comment, which Mr. Kerry claimed with some justification was an off-the-cuff muddle (a "botched joke") of remarks he intended to give, was swift and acidic. The *Wall Street Journal* quipped that late-night comedians "knelt down and gave thanks yesterday for the gift of Senator John Kerry, whose cultural condescension keeps on giving."[36] The newspaper concluded that Sen. Kerry "was saying that only fools and knaves, not patriots, end up fighting in Iraq." The *Washington Times* joked that

"Mr. Kerry gives elitism a bad name."[37] The most original response came from a group of soldiers in Iraq, who had themselves photographed holding up a hastily painted sign: HALP US JON CARRY— WE R STUCK HEAR N IRAK. That's how they printed it, except that the k in "stuck" was turned backwards. For several days, the Right feasted and the Left ran for cover.

But did the senator really smear soldiers? Given his past record of ill-considered and even outrageous comments, it was hard not to jump to that conclusion. However, within a short time after his "botched joke" (and after he had lashed out at his critics as politically motivated), his office released the written text of his remarks, from which he had apparently varied (several different newspaper sources gave different versions):

> I can't overstress the importance of a great education. Do you know where you end up if you don't study, if you aren't smart, if you're intellectually lazy? You end up getting us stuck in a war in Iraq. Just ask President Bush.[38]

Clearly, what Kerry actually said was not a premeditated attack on our armed forces. And yet, as I wrote at the time (on the Compass Points blog):

> The fact remains it's [his prepared speech] not what he actually said and his grin after saying what he did say—and the laughter from his audience—was easily taken to be a slam against the troops.[39]

Kerry certainly learned a lesson from this slip. In explaining his vote on the appropriations bill in May 2007, he said:

We support the troops by getting the policy right and this bill allows the President to keep getting the policy wrong. We need a deadline to force Iraqis to stand up for Iraq and bring our heroes home, not watered down benchmarks and blank check waivers for this President. We support the troops by funding the right mission, not with a White House that opposes a pay raise for our brave men and women in uniform.[40]

"If a young fellow has an option . . ."

But if John Kerry does not believe that our fighting men and women are dumb, other left-wingers seem to. Just a few weeks after Sen. Kerry's "botched joke," New York congressman Charlie Rangel chose to step into the same mud puddle. Appearing on the *Fox News Sunday* television program, Rep. Rangel said of the men and women serving in America's armed forces:

> If there's anyone who believes that these youngsters want to fight, as the Pentagon and some generals have said, you can forget about it. No bright individual wants to fight just because of a bonus and just because of educational benefits. And most all of them come from communities of very, very high unemployment.[41]

Rangel was responding to a question about his call for the reinstatement of a military draft. Rangel believes this is important because he thinks—as suggested in the above quote—that poor and uneducated young people are represented disproportionately in the military, and because he believes that, since the draft would bring the sons (and daughters) of the wealthy and well-educated into the armed forces, it would temporize the nation's impulse to go to war. (As an editorial in *Investor's Business Daily* put it on Memorial Day 2005, the all-volunteer force made antiwar rallies vanish. "Now . . . the anti-war crowd doesn't throw tantrums. It writes headlines."[42])

Rep. Rangel went on to say:

If a young fellow has an option of having a decent career or joining the Army to fight in Iraq, you can bet your life that he would not be in Iraq. . . . those who have the least opportunities at this age find themselves in the military, as I did when I was 18 years old.[43]

However, a Heritage Foundation study indicates otherwise:

U.S. military recruits are more similar than dissimilar to the American youth population. The slight differences are that wartime U.S. military enlistees are better educated, wealthier, and more rural on average than their civilian peers.[44]

Indeed, the only population group from which enlistments are declining is the poor: down from 18 percent in 1999 to 13.7 percent in 2005.[45] And to the extent that Rangel, who is black, is implying something concerning race, it must be noted that, as the United States Defense Department recently reported:

African Americans represented about 17 percent of the force [and] accounted for 11 percent of deaths [in Iraq]. On the other hand, whites accounted for 67 percent of the force, and suffered 74 percent of deaths. The corresponding numbers for Hispanics were 9 and 11 percent.[46]

Surely Congressman Rangel is familiar with these facts. Ever since he began his call for a draft, these statistics have been made clear to him—often to his face, as on the Fox program. Some think it isn't simply that he believes rich, white folks will put their foot down about a given conflict if *their* kids have to fight, but that he believes the Vietnam War was ended *because* there was a draft—that the "youngsters" who were called upon to fight brought an end to the conflict through their protests. To be sure, there have been demonstrations over the war in Iraq, but it's fair to say there's been nothing on the scale the nation saw in the late sixties and early seventies. And so the way to bring back mass protests is to bring back the draft.

More so even than Sen. Kerry, Rep. Rangel quickly became the subject of protests himself. James Taranto of the *Wall Street Journal* devoted a substantial portion of his Best of the Web blog during several days at the end of 2006 to what he termed "Responding to Rangel." Most of the e-mails and letters Taranto posted came from veterans who were, in the words of the American Legion's National Commander, angry at "Rangel's view of our troops [which] couldn't be further from the truth. . . ."[47]

One young naval officer wrote to Taranto:

I think . . . Rep. Rangel's [comments] reveal not only the mindset of liberal policy makers in relation to the military, but also their view of what I like to call "duty to the self." Those that achieve the greatest academic achievement usually tend to be the most self-centered. . . . Why should someone give up four years (or more!) of comfort and high earning potential to be subjected to months away from family, cramped living conditions, and the legally binding order of others?[48]

The officer answers the question with his service to the nation. But what about Sen. Kerry and Rep. Rangel? Both are veterans (Rangel served in the army) and public servants of many years, ones we might expect to know enough of our nation's history to recognize not only the virtue of military service but also its necessity.

Hitler and Company

In the case of Mr. Kerry's Senate colleague Richard Durbin of Illinois, reelection to the World's Greatest Deliberative Body in 2008 may depend on his ability to overcome a very serious smear against the armed forces.

Sen. Durbin is the senior United States senator from the Land of Lincoln. In 2004, he was elected by his Democratic senatorial colleagues to the position of whip, which is to say second in command of his party's business in the Senate. This was before he compared the U.S. armed forces' treatment of suspected al Qaeda terrorists imprisoned at Guantánamo Bay with the practices of Hitler's Germany, Stalin's Soviet Union, and Pol Pot's Cambodia.

Standing on the floor of the Senate on June 14, 2005, Durbin read the text of an FBI agent's e-mail:

When you read some of the graphic descriptions of what has occurred here—I almost hesitate to put them in the record, and yet they have to be added to this debate. Let me read to you what one FBI agent saw. And I quote from his [actually, her] report:

"On a couple of occasions, I entered interview rooms to find a detainee chained hand and foot in a fetal position to the floor, with no chair, food or water. Most times they urinated or defecated on themselves, and had been left there for 18–24 hours or more. On one occasion, the air conditioning had been turned down so far and the temperature was so cold in the room, that the barefooted detainee was shaking with cold. . . . On another occasion, the [air conditioner] had been turned off, making the temperature in the unventilated room well over 100 degrees. The detainee was almost unconscious on the floor, with a pile of hair next to him. He had apparently been literally pulling his hair out throughout the night. On another occasion, not only was the temperature unbearably hot, but extremely loud rap music was being played in the room, and had been since the day before, with the detainee chained hand and foot in the fetal position on the tile floor."

If I read this to you and did not tell you that it was an FBI agent describing what Americans had done to prisoners in their control, you would most certainly believe this must have been done by Nazis, Soviets in their gulags, or some mad regime—Pol Pot or others—that had no concern for human beings. Sadly, that is not the case. This was the action of Americans in the treatment of their prisoners.[49]

This raised a firestorm, not least in the Senate itself. Durbin's colleague John Warner, chairman of the Senate Armed Services

Committee, pointed out that the e-mail Durbin had read was a raw FBI report, which had not been investigated. The following month, Air Force Lt. Gen. Randall M. Schmidt issued his formal report. Investigators had not been able to substantiate any of the FBI agent's specific claims, he wrote. In all, they found no evidence of torture, though they did find cases of "aggressive interrogations" of suspected al Qaeda and Taliban terrorists.[50]

Meanwhile, Durbin had apologized, saying he "never intended any disrespect" to U.S. troops.[51] But the smear against our military serving in Guantánamo had been made, and it had its effect on soldiers, Marines, sailors, and airmen.

Negative reaction to Durbin's comments was swift, but came mostly from the military and the blogosphere—not from mainstream media. For many newspaper and television reporters, the Senator's hyperbole simply offered an opportunity to report about what the media considered abuse, even torture, of Muslim prisoners. And turning it around the other way, Sen. Durbin, not known as one of the Senate's more reflective or philosophical members, may just have been taking his cue from the media. A few days before Durbin's speech, Bob Schieffer, anchor of the *CBS Evening News*, compared Gitmo to the Hanoi Hilton—the prison where John McCain, Everett Alvarez, James Stockdale, and many other American POWs were held and tortured during the Vietnam War.[52]

As a guest on *Imus in the Morning*, Schieffer told of watching the A&E film about John McCain's suffering in Hanoi.

[It] made me rethink this whole thing about how we treat these prisoners in Guantánamo. And people keep making this point, this is so bad for us in the Arab world, this is giving us such a bad name. My problem with it is, what's it doing to us? Do we want our kids to think we're that kind of people, that we participate in things like this? And if you see this film . . . about John McCain and what he went through, it's putting it in reverse.[53]

The negative reporting in the press did not stop with Durbin's apology. For instance, two months later, in August 2005, *Editor & Publisher* magazine reported on a speech by American Legion commander Thomas P. Cadmus, an army vet, in which he pledged that the Legion would "stand against anyone and any group that would demoralize our troops, or worse, endanger their lives by encouraging terrorists to continue their cowardly attacks against freedom loving peoples." Here's how *Editor & Publisher* reported the speech:

> The American Legion, which has 2.7-million members, has declared war on antiwar protesters, and the media could be next. Speaking at its national convention in Honolulu, the group's national commander called for an end to all "public protests" and "media events" against the war, even though they are protected by the Bill of Rights.[54]

At no point had Commander Cadmus called for anything of the sort. Quite to the contrary, he said that nobody "respects the right to protest more than one who has fought for it," and simply stated his hope that protestors would express their dissent through the political process rather than through the kind of print and broadcast stories that undermine morale. Perhaps Commander Cadmus was thinking of the "media riot" (as Mark Steyn might put it) that had erupted over the prisoner-abuse scandals at Abu Ghraib prison in Iraq in 2004.

It must be stipulated that there was abuse at Abu Ghraib. There can be no doubt about this, since some of the American soldiers charged with humiliating and even torturing Iraqi detainees were stupid enough to have made a photographic record of their crimes.

But, again, as in My Lai, there is the matter of proportion. First, like the My Lai Massacre, the abuses at Abu Ghraib were not U.S. policy. Far from it: As soon as military authorities heard rumors of the abuse, they launched an investigation. Eventually, four soldiers were formally charged under the Uniform Code of Military Justice with detainee abuse. Two of them were convicted and sentenced to terms in prison (three years for one of the soldiers, ten for the other).

Second—as in the case of My Lai versus Hué City—the few cases of abuse or even murder committed by American forces pale in comparison to the butchery of those against whom those troops have been fighting. Much of the discussion about Abu Ghraib simply ignored the more serious abuse that had occurred there during the reign of Saddam Hussein. Christopher Hitchens offered a corrective: "Before March 2003, Abu Ghraib was an abattoir, a torture chamber, and a concentration camp. Now, without reason, it is an international byword for Yankee imperialism and sadism." [55]

Yet the press continues to make bigger headlines of every splinter in American policy while minimizing the Sequoia of terrorism. Consider simply the evolution of journalistic language from 9/11 forward. By the time the Abu Ghraib scandal became public, which occurred a year after the successful Coalition invasion of Iraq, "terrorists" had in some media outlets become "the insurgency" and in still others "resistance fighters," with the evocation of World War II and the implication that Coalition forces = Nazis.[56] Sen. Durbin may have felt blindsided by the adverse reaction to his remarks, since they were no different from the editorial positions of a number of major American media outlets. After all, the *New York Times* ran the Abu Ghraib story on its front page for thirty-two consecutive days.[57]

But, as William J. Bennett said at a speech in Palm Springs, California, in 2004:

> One must judge this democracy—ours—as one must judge any country—democracy or not: in its totality, and in its mean. Not in its extreme, and not in its aberration. Although we should be proud of how we are treating our aberrant soldiers, with accountability and due process and punishment, I agree with what the late Pat Moynihan said. He asked then, and we ask now: "Am I ashamed to speak on behalf of a less than perfect country? Find me a better one. Do I suppose there are societies which are free of sin? No, I don't. Do I think ours is, on balance, incomparably the most hopeful set of human relations the world has? Yes, I do. Have we done obscene things? Yes, we have. How did our people learn about them? They learned about them on television and in the newspapers." And we put our criminals—whether in uniform or not—on trial.[58]

As for the prisoner "abuses" at Guantánamo—that story as much as any demonstrates the utter animosity of the press toward the military. In its May 9, 2005, issue, *Newsweek* magazine accused an Army interrogator at Gitmo of flushing a copy of the Koran down a cell toilet, among other even more lurid details:

> Investigators probing interrogation abuses at the U.S. detention center at Guantánamo Bay have confirmed some infractions alleged in internal FBI e-mails that surfaced late last year. Among the previously unreported cases, sources tell *Newsweek*: interrogators, in an attempt to rattle suspects, flushed a Qur'an down a toilet and led a detainee around with a collar and dog leash. An Army spokesman confirms that 10 Gitmo interrogators have already been disciplined for mistreating prisoners, including one woman who took off her top, rubbed her finger through a detainee's hair and sat on the detainee's lap. (New details of sexual abuse—including an instance in which a female interrogator allegedly wiped her red-stained hand on a detainee's face, telling him it was her menstrual blood—are also in a new book to be published this week by a former Gitmo translator.)

The magazine's reporters, Michael Isikoff and John Barry, alleged that the story was based on FBI e-mails and a soon-to-be-published report on the prison from U.S. Southern Command. Trouble is, there were no such e-mails and no such language in the SouthCom report. This would have been just your garden-variety smear of the military were it not for the fact that the *Newsweek* story sparked riots in Muslim nations that led to the deaths of more than a dozen people. As the editors of *National Review* wrote ten days later—after *Newsweek* retracted its false story—the whole incident was connected "to the media's general frenzy over Abu Ghraib," and to the media's unwillingness to credit the fact that terrorists are explicitly instructed (specifically, in a captured al Qaeda training manual) that if captured they are to make up stories to embarrass their captors.

It was never entirely credible in any case that a thick book could have been flushed down a latrine, but *Newsweek* wanted the story to be true and so ran it. Subsequent investigations showed that there *had* been some "Koran abuse" at Gitmo:

> [F]ive cases, including one in which a detainee complained that his Koran had been kicked, and another in which urine from a guard relieving himself accidentally blew into an air vent and onto a Koran below.
>
> That's it.[59]

It's interesting to note that the SouthCom report also found fifteen cases of Koran abuse *by Muslim detainees*. "These included using a Quran as a pillow, ripping pages out of the Quran, attempting to flush a Quran down the toilet and urinating on the Quran."[60]

On January 30, 2007, *Washington Post* columnist and blogger William M. Arkin wrote that complaints by members of the armed forces about criticism from home were misplaced. (A number of men serving in Iraq had expressed such concerns to *NBC Nightly News* shortly before Arkin wrote his piece.) In fact, he wrote,

> I'm all for everyone expressing their opinion, even those who wear the uniform of the United States Army. But I also hope that military commanders took the soldiers aside after the story and explained to them why it wasn't for them to disapprove of the American people.[61]

Arkin went on:

> These soldiers should be grateful that the American public,
> which by all polls overwhelmingly disapproves of the Iraq
> war and the President's handling of it, do still offer their
> support to them, and their respect.
>
> Through every Abu Ghraib and Haditha, through every
> rape and murder, the American public has indulged those in
> uniform, accepting that the incidents were the product of bad
> apples or even of some administration or command order. . . .
>
> Sure it is the junior enlisted men who go to jail, but even
> at anti-war protests, the focus is firmly on the White House
> and the policy. We just don't see very many "baby killer" epi-
> thets being thrown around these days, no one in uniform is
> being spit upon.

Arkin even goes so far as to indulge a little fantasy about a military coup in the United States:

> I can imagine some post-9/11 moment, when the American
> people say enough already with the wars against terrorism
> and those in the national security establishment feel these
> same frustrations. In my little parable, those in leadership
> positions shake their heads that the people don't get it, that
> they don't understand that the threat from terrorism, while
> difficult to defeat, demands commitment and sacrifice and is
> very real because it is so shadowy, that the very survival of
> the United States is at stake. Those Hoovers and Nixons will
> use these kids in uniform as their soldiers. If it weren't the
> United States, I'd say the story ends with a military coup

where those in the know, and those with fire in their bellies, save the nation from the people.

But it is the United States and instead this NBC report is just an ugly reminder of the price we pay for a mercenary— oops sorry, volunteer—force that thinks it is doing the dirty work.

It was hardly surprising that Arkin's smear of soldiers was met with anger—from other journalists, from bloggers, from cartoonists, and from the troops themselves. Indeed, he was quite overwhelmed by the negative reaction. On February 6, he wrote that the messages he received from people in the military were "the most respectful and reflective," but that much of the rest of the reaction was "biting, fanatical, threatening" and demonstrated "the worst of polarized and hate-filled America." He cites no specifics, but I can imagine that he was the subject of some very intense criticism—though whether it is America or Arkin that is "hate-filled" is another question.

Mother Sheehan and Absolute Moral Authority

The loss of a son in battle is a tragedy from which most parents would find it difficult to recover. Through all the wars in which Americans have fought, the ultimate sacrifice of one's child is hard to accept as a consequence of war policy—no matter how valid is that policy or how broad-based is its support.

The parents of former National Football League star Pat Tillman—who gave up a lucrative career in sports to serve his country and who lost his life in action in Afghanistan—were understandably angry when it turned out that the army's initial report of the circumstance surrounding their son's death was wrong. In fact, it appeared that the army had intentionally withheld the sickening truth that Sgt. Tillman had been killed by "friendly fire."

But before the revelation of those circumstances, liberal columnist and cartoonist Ted Rall had portrayed Tillman not as a patriotic hero but as a killer.[62] In a four-panel cartoon, he speculates: Was Tillman an idiot, a sap, or a hero?

It's clear—from the cartoon and from his other writing (in which he has compared George W. Bush to Hitler and Stalin)—which of these sentiments Rall rejects.

But the frustration and anger expressed by Pat Tillman's parents and family is nothing compared to the rage of Casey Sheehan's mother. Army Spc. Sheehan was killed in Iraq, and his mother, Cindy, has been much in the news ever since.

Of her anti-Bush protests, *New York Times* columnist Maureen Dowd famously wrote that "the moral authority of parents who bury children killed in Iraq is absolute."[63] This is absurd on the face of it, since many parents who have lost children in the war support positions opposite those of Mrs. Sheehan, but Dowd was making a point in support of her own opposition to what she calls the "Bushies."* She writes that they tried to discredit Sheehan, who was demanding a second meeting with the commander in chief, by pointing out that the grieving mother had said kind things about the president after their first get-together.

---

*About Dowd's standards of accuracy, her paper's own ombudsman wrote that she "was still writing that Alberto R. Gonzales 'called the Geneva Conventions *quaint*'" nearly two months after a correction in the news pages noted that Gonzales had specifically applied the term to Geneva provisions about commissary privileges, athletic uniforms and scientific instruments" (*New York Times*, May 22, 2005).

But this is the sort of thing Mrs. Sheehan had taken to saying since:

> Last weekend, Karl Rove said that I was a clown and the anti-war movement was "non-existent." I wonder if the hundreds of thousands of people who showed up today to protest this war and George's failed policies know that they don't exist. It is also so incredible to me that Karl thinks that he can wish us away by saying we aren't real. Well, Karl and Co., we are real, we do exist and we are not going away until this illegal and immoral occupation of Iraq is over and you are sent back to the depths of whatever slimy, dark, and loathsome place you came from. I may be a clown, Karl, but you are about to be indicted. You also preside over one of the biggest three-ring, malevolent circuses of all time: the Bush administration.[64]

Or take this sample, from her report on her sixteen-day tour of Europe, titled "Friends Don't Let Friends Commit War Crimes":

> I believe Bush and Blair are too far gone for redemption. They both need to be removed from power and tried for their war crimes and betrayals. Until they are removed, the murder and the mayhem will continue.
>
> In Ireland, I met with that country's equivalent of Condi Rice, the dignified Foreign Minister Dermot Ahern. As a matter of fact, he had just met with the "steely" Condi the week before. Incredibly, he accepted assurances from her that the CIA airplanes (up to 60 documented by peace activists) that are landing in Shannon airport are not trans-

porting prisoners for extraordinary rendition (i.e., torture). That's like accepting a pirate's assurance that he's not going to steal your boat as he's boarding it with a drawn sword! I tried to impress on Mr. Ahern that the leaders of my government are known pathological liars, and can't be believed on this or anything. The torture planes are landing on Irish soil, so Ireland should inspect them for human rights violations. If Condi and her "husband" George aren't doing anything wrong, they have nothing to be concerned with.[65]

Or this, on her "resignation" from active duty in the antiwar movement:

Good-bye America . . . you are not the country that I love and I finally realized no matter how much I sacrifice, I can't make you be that country unless you want it.
It's up to you now.[66]

Columnist Christopher Hitchens aptly tagged Mrs. Sheehan's method when he wrote: "Sheehan has obviously taken a short course in the Michael Moore/Ramsey Clark school of Iraq analysis and has not succeeded in making it one atom more elegant or persuasive."[67]

We're All Soldiers Now

Of our soldiers, it remains to say simply that they stand in our stead in the battle for liberty itself. As Peggy Noonan wrote in the *Wall Street Journal* less than a month after the 9/11 attacks, we're all soldiers now. "Think," she wrote. "We're at war; think like a warrior and a survivor. This is not only a good idea, it will make you feel better, or at least a little bit safer, which is not a bad way to feel."[68]

But the press has not helped Americans think in that way. Many will argue that it is not their job to rally round the flag, and there is truth in this, but it is also not their job to desecrate the flag and those who fight to defend it. Consider this from author and professor James Q. Wilson:

> When the Center for Media and Public Affairs made a non-partisan evaluation of network news broadcasts, it found that during the active war against Saddam Hussein, 51% of the reports about the conflict were negative. Six months after the battle had ended, 77% were negative; in the 2004 general election, 89% were negative; by the spring of 2006, 94% were negative.[69]

Why? Prof. Wilson concludes that it's because the ownership and management of mainstream media are antiwar. Intentional or not, the effect on the morale of the armed forces and the reality of coverage is the same: soldiers know they have been smeared. Facts have been manipulated in order to portray them in the worst possible light.

One wonders what mainstream media imagine would happen if pride in the profession of arms were diminished to the point that nobody would think it honorable to enlist. Where would their treasured freedoms be then?

IV

SMEARING THE FAITHFUL

They are the real American Taliban—the Christian Coalition, Gary Bauer, The 700 Club and Focus on the Family, the Catholic cardinals—forcing their way into politics and believing their religious beliefs should be the law of the land.

—Michelangelo Signorile, author of
Queer in America *and co-founding*
editor of OutWeek magazine[1]

THERE CAN BE NO DOUBT THAT we are living through an era in which many of society's most treasured assumptions are being called into question. This is in no case as true as in the matter of religion.

And it's not simply an extension of the critiques of Karl Marx (that religion is a drug that stupefies the common folk) or Friedrich Nietzsche (that the modern world's hubristic self-regard rejects God)—though it certainly embraces both of those things—but that the faithful are now considered actually either idiotic or demonic. The epigraph for this chapter comes after Signorile*

---

*We met him in Chapter 2 and considered his gleeful smear of the late Cardinal Spellman, which he would presumably justify, as he justified "outing" in general, on the grounds that "invisibility and the closet were hurting the gay movement and adversely affecting the AIDS epidemic."

has evoked Islamofascist beheadings of homosexuals—explicitly in Saudi Arabia and implicitly under the former regime in Afghanistan. He then says:

> Why is it still considered a crime in Texas for people to engage in sex in the privacy of their own homes?
>
> Well, for the same reason that Saudi Arabia slices off the heads of homosexuals: because some religious fanatics believe homosexuality is bad, and the powers that be kowtow to those religious extremists.

He is making the same sort of moral-equivalency argument familiar from the days when the liberal appraisal of American capitalism asserted its similarity—as a power structure—to Soviet communism; this despite the fact that none of those listed in Signorile's bill of indictment has ever advocated anything more than cleaving to their traditional understanding of human sexuality. But Signorile's indictment of the faithful is hardly uncommon or out of the mainstream today. As Patrick Hynes points out in his fine book *In Defense of the Religious Right*, liberal intolerance toward religion, and especially conservative Christianity, is very much in vogue.[2] Here are some of the more egregious recent examples:

- In a speech at Tufts University two weeks after the 2004 election, Andy Rooney of *60 Minutes* attributed the victory of Bush and congressional Republicans to the votes of Christian fundamentalists, and in turn attributed the fundamentalists' religious beliefs to "a lack of education. They haven't been exposed to what the world has to offer."[3]

• The *Washington Post*'s Michael Weisskopf produced an
  analysis of the political clout of the "religious right" (which
  he also refers to interchangeably as "fundamentalists,"
  "evangelicals," and "the gospel lobby"), in which he wrote:

  > Unlike other powerful interests, [the religious right]
  > does not lavish campaign funds on candidates for
  > Congress nor does it entertain them. The strength of
  > fundamentalist leaders lies in their flocks. Corporations
  > pay public relations firms millions of dollars to contrive
  > the kind of grass-roots response that [Rev. Jerry] Fal-
  > well or Pat Robertson can galvanize in a televised ser-
  > mon. Their followers are largely poor, uneducated and
  > easy to command.[4]

  The next day, perhaps demonstrating the truth of one part
  of Weisskopf's assertion—that the religious Right can mo-
  bilize itself quickly and powerfully—the *Post* ran the following "Correction": "An article yesterday characterized followers
  of television evangelists Jerry Falwell and Pat Robertson as
  'largely poor, uneducated and easy to command.' There is no
  factual basis for that statement.")

• In his remarks upon receiving the Global Environmental
  Citizen Award from the Center for Health and the Global
  Environment at Harvard Medical School in December 2004,
  PBS commentator Bill Moyers described the beliefs of those
  Christians who look forward to Armageddon as the means of
  bringing on the "end times" and implied that all conservative
  Christians, and all candidates who court their votes, share
  these beliefs:

One of the biggest changes in politics in my lifetime is that the delusional is no longer marginal. It has come in from the fringe, to sit in the seat of power in the Oval Office and in Congress.

For the first time in our history, ideology and theology hold a monopoly of power in Washington. Theology asserts propositions that cannot be proven true; ideologues hold stoutly to a worldview despite being contradicted by what is generally accepted as reality. The offspring of ideology and theology are not always bad but they are always blind. And that is the danger: voters and politicians alike, oblivious to the facts.

One-third of the American electorate, if a recent Gallup Poll is accurate, believes the Bible is literally true. This past November, several million good and decent citizens went to the polls believing in what is known as the "rapture index."[5]

Whether it is the controversy over so-called Intelligent Design versus the Darwinian theory of evolution or the results of the 2004 presidential election, in which "values voters" helped to give George W. Bush more votes than any other candidate in history, the liberal mantra is the same: *It's the stupids, stupid*. And the mainstream media cleverly use parallel terminology to smear American Christians: The people who support Intelligent Design and Mr. Bush are *fundamentalists*; the terrorists who daily murder civilians in Iraq are *fundamentalists*. And some people on the Left make the linkage even more explicit. Thus Michelangelo Signorile, quoted above, and thus Rosie O'Donnell on ABC's *The View*: "Radical Christianity is just as threatening as radical Islam in a country like America where we have separation of church and state."[6]

And thus a man who came close to becoming president of the United States, Al Gore. Talking with *The New Yorker* editor David Remnick about the faith of George W. Bush, the former vice president said: "It's a particular kind of religiosity. It's the American version of the same fundamentalist impulse that we see in Saudi Arabia, in Kashmir . . . It's the vengeance, the brimstone."[7]

Even Republican senator John McCain has called religious conservatives "agents of ignorance,"[8] and another GOP stalwart, Rep. Christopher Shays of Connecticut, has claimed: "This Republican Party of Lincoln has become a party of theocracy."[9]

No wonder that more than half (56 percent) of atheists and agnostics think "radical Christianity" is just as threatening in the United States as "radical Islam," according to a poll conducted by the Barna Group in California.[10]

A very low point in liberal opinion about conservative Christians came from the pen of columnist Paul Krugman of the *New York Times* on March 29, 2005, when he compared religious conservatives who opposed withdrawing food from Terri Schiavo to Islamic militants. (Schiavo was the Florida woman whose persistent vegetative state had begun in 1990 and ended with her death two days after Krugman's column was published.) Krugman wrote: "America isn't yet a place where liberal politicians, and even conservatives who aren't sufficiently hard-line, fear assassination. But unless moderates take a stand against the growing power of domestic extremists, it can happen here."[11]

That's an alarmist assertion for which the columnist cites no evidence. This shows him to be a polemicist. But another statement in the same article reveals the smear artist at work: "One thing that's going on is a climate of fear for those who try to enforce laws that religious extremists oppose. Randall Terry, a spokesman for Terri Schiavo's parents, hasn't killed anyone, but one of his former close associates in the anti-abortion movement is serving time for murdering a doctor."

Now, Terry has had an interesting career. As founder of Operation Rescue, the anti-abortion group, he has been the subject of controversy: he was sued successfully under the federal Racketeer-Influenced and Corrupt Organizations Act (RICO) by the National Organization of Women, which sought to stop Operation Rescue demonstrations outside abortion clinics (the lower court's decision was later overturned by the Supreme Court); he ran a divisive campaign for Congress in upstate New York and lost; he has been accused of sexual improprieties and been censured by his own church.

In short, Randall Terry may be an extremely unlikable fellow, but there is scant evidence that he is one of those who really would trash the Constitution in pursuit of an American theocracy. But Krugman's phrase "hasn't killed anyone" is a classic smear tactic.

In making the charge, Krugman is simply repeating a tangential association made earlier in his own newspaper. On July 20, 2001, the *New York Times* reported that one of Terry's "most avid followers in Binghamton [New York] was James E. [actually, James C.] Kopp, now charged in the 1998 murder of a doctor who performed abortions in Buffalo." The *Times* goes on to say that when Terry drove from New York to Georgia to take part in an abortion protest, Kopp also made the trip (in another vehicle); that when Terry was arrested, Kopp "followed him to jail," where he "adhered to Mr. Terry's orders"; and that after his release

Kopp returned to New York to "work alongside Mr. Terry. . . ." Nowhere in any of this is there the slightest suggestion that at any point or in any way did Terry incite Kopp to murder, nor for that matter is there any actual demonstration that Kopp was a "close associate," to use Krugman's phrase. And even if he were, how exactly does that link Terry to the murder? Has Terry been charged with abetting the crime? Krugman was no doubt a close associate of Jayson Blair, the *Times* reporter dismissed by the paper for plagiarism and fabrication in stories he wrote for the newspaper. Does the Blair association taint Krugman's writing?*

As we'll see in this book's final chapter, the religious Right (Randall Terry excepted) is simply closer in its points of view to America's heritage than is the secular Left. But is conservative Christianity—theocratic or otherwise—really ascendant in America?

The spate of recent religious films in Hollywood, such as Ron Maxwell's *Gods and Generals*, Mel Gibson's *The Passion of the Christ*, and Andrew Adamson's *The Chronicles of Narnia: The Lion, the Witch and the Wardrobe*, marked an exception to a longstanding trend of hostility toward religion in American film. Most films that depict faith (and there are a lot) show it as an oppressive force, the refuge of nutty people—sometimes even the criminally insane. Some of these are as seemingly innocent as the comedy *Saved!*, about a girl at a conservative Christian high school who discovers she is pregnant "and searches for support from other students that have been similarly rejected by the student

---

*The *New York Times* public editor, Daniel Okrent, wrote of Krugman that he "has the disturbing habit of shaping, slicing and selectively citing numbers that pleases his acolytes but leaves him open to substantive assaults" (May 22, 2005).

body because of their religion or disability," in the words of United Artists' press release—which describes the film as "sweetly subversive." Others have nothing sweet about them, but intend to be quite subversive—notably *The Beast*, by the self-described "former fundamentalist Christian" Brian Flemming. Its promotional material describes it this way:

> When her father, a biblical scholar, mysteriously disappears, a Christian high-school student named Danielle investigates. She discovers that he had stumbled across a cover-up of Christianity's best-kept secret: that Jesus Christ never existed.
>
> Now that she possesses proof of this dangerous fact, Danielle must confront two strong forces: a band of fundamentalist Christians who will stop at nothing to suppress the truth, and her own desire for Jesus Christ to be real.[12]

Other movies from recent years that are in one way or another anti-Christian include *The Book of Daniel*, *South Park: The Movie*, *Hail Mary*, *Dogma*, *The Last Temptation of Christ*, *V for Vendetta*, and *The Da Vinci Code*, of which last we'll hear more in a minute. (It was a curious fact that many of these films did quite poorly at the box office, whereas the films depicting faith in a positive way often do very well. Could it be that the producers and directors of the former aren't really in it for the money after all?)

Meanwhile, a look at the list of best-selling books of 2006 on Amazon.com could be interpreted as indicating that the religious Right is actually on the ropes in the USA. In fact, traditional, conservative Christianity isn't about to throw in the towel, but there are certainly a lot of punches being thrown by its opponents.

Start with the hugely successful *The Da Vinci Code* (Doubleday, 2003) by Dan Brown, which by the end of 2006 was enjoying its third consecutive year atop the best-seller lists thanks to its reincarnation as "a major motion picture." And it was high on the list in three—make that *four*—different editions: hardcover, trade paperback, mass-market paperback, and even a Special Illustrated Edition. Brown's book follows (closely enough to generate an unsuccessful lawsuit) the scenario outlined by another best seller, back on the list again after more than twenty years. The tale spun in its predecessor, the purportedly nonfiction *Holy Blood, Holy Grail* (Delacorte Press, 1982, 2005), suggested that Jesus did not die in the Crucifixion, but was spirited away by his disciples to France, where he wed Mary Magdalene and sired the Merovingian dynasty. Also at or near the top of the list were a number of *Da Vinci Code/Holy Blood* clones: *The Secret Supper* (Atria Books, 2006), *The Templar Revelation* (Bantam Press, 1997), *The Templar Legacy* (Ballantine Books, 2006), *Map of Bones* (Morrow, 2005), *The Sion Revelation* (Simon & Schuster, 2006), and *The Jesus Dynasty* (Simon & Schuster, 2006), to name just six. One of the three authors of *Holy Blood, Holy Grail*, Michael Baigent, scored big with *The Jesus Papers* (HarperSanFrancisco, 2006, which was released just as his suit against Brown reached the court.

In addition to these fictional and fanciful attacks on Christian orthodoxy, there were also some more serious nonfiction books that question traditional Protestant (especially evangelical and fundamentalist) and Roman Catholic understandings of Christ and the church. Among them:

- *Misquoting Jesus* (HarperSanFrancisco, 2005), by liberal New Testament scholar Bart D. Ehrman, whose *The Lost Gospel of*

Judas Iscariot (Oxford University Press, 2006)—about the so-called Gospel of Judas—was also on the list. Here is a sample of Ehrman's thought: "Sometimes Christian apologists say there are only three options to who Jesus was: a liar, a lunatic or the Lord. But there could be a fourth option— legend."[13]

- *The Theocons: Secular America Under Siege*, (Doubleday, 2006) by Damon Linker, a former employee of Fr. Richard John Neuhaus: "At its core, the Bush administration's overt religiosity represents the triumph of an ideological movement that for the past several decades has devoted itself to fashioning a theocratic governing philosophy for the United States—a governing philosophy rooted in Roman Catholicism. Led by Father Richard John Neuhaus, this group of "theoconservatives" has actively sought to roll back the division of church and state in American life."[14]

- *What Jesus Meant* (Viking, 2006), by Garry Wills, often described as a "critical Catholic": "Pope Benedict XVI, like his predecessors, is returning to the religion that Jesus renounced, with all its paraphernalia of priesthood."[15]

- *Breaking the Spell* (Viking, 2006), by Daniel C. Dennett: "The belief that belief in God is so important that it must not be subjected to the risks of disconfirmation or serious criticism has led the devout to "save" their beliefs by making them incomprehensible even to themselves."[16]

- *The Jesus Dynasty*, by James Tabor, which says the father of Jesus was certainly not God and probably not Joseph, but a Roman soldier: "Properly understood, it [the hidden story of Jesus' parentage] changes everything we thought we knew about Jesus, his mission, and his message."[17]

- *The Baptizing of America: The Religious Right's Plans for the*

Rest of Us (Thunder's Mouth Press, 2006), by James Rudin, whose ominous subtitle just about says it all: "We can judge people by their deeds. The Christocrats' deeds are really an attack on public schools, on libraries, and the media. They attack the existing structures and then try to have them replaced with Christocratic libraries, Christocratic public schools or academies, or Christocratic media. . . . That's the strategy—to destroy the existing structure, or discredit it, and then try to replace it—using federal, state or local public money to support their schools or their unique libraries."[18]

- *Thy Kingdom Come: How the Religious Right Distorts the Faith and Threatens America: An Evangelical's Lament* (Basic Books, 2006), by Randall Balmer: "I write as a jilted lover. The evangelical faith that nurtured me as a child and sustains me as an adult has been hijacked by right-wing zealots."[19]

- *Kingdom Coming: The Rise of Christian Nationalism* (W.W. Norton & Co., 2006), by Michelle Goldberg: "I was terrified by America's increasing hostility to . . . cosmopolitan values."[20]

- *American Fascists: The Christian Right and the War on America* (Free Press, 2006), by Chris Hedges, a former *New York Times* stalwart: "My argument is that this [the "dominionist movement"] is not a religious movement. Although it certainly depends on the support of many earnest, well-meaning, decent people who are religious, I would argue that they are manipulated not only, of course, to be fleeced for their own money, but essentially to give up moral choice and surrender to the authoritarian demands of these leaders [James Dobson, Pat Robertson, and Jerry Falwell, who was still alive when Hedges's book was published] to march forward and essentially dismantle our democratic state. And I think that when we look closely at what it is that this Christian right movement espouses, it does bear many similarities to the main pillars of fascist movements. . . ."[21]

And, believe me, this is just a partial list. As Ross Douthat, an editor at *Atlantic Monthly*, observed recently: "This is a paranoid moment in American politics."[22]

And of all the suspicious, fearful, and even obsessed best sellers, none was bigger or more stinging in its criticisms of American conservative Christianity than *American Theocracy* by Kevin Phillips.

Subtitled "The Peril and Politics of Radical Religion, Oil, and Borrowed Money in the 21st Century," *American Theocracy* asserts that most of America's popular and fastest-growing religious institutions and many of our famous and widely admired Christian leaders are dedicated to the establishment of a theocracy: to what, if true, would certainly seem to be an unconstitutional intermingling of religion and law.

The question is: *Is there any truth to this?*

If so, we face wrenching internecine conflicts in the near feature. Not an Apocalypse, perhaps, but dreadful and agonizing nonetheless.

If not, then those men and women whom Phillips—and many other writers and bloggers—have accused of being theocrats are the subjects of an extremely energetic smear campaign.

In the book's preface, Phillips makes his point succinctly. (As indicated in the subtitle, the book's three-pronged attack also aims at the Bush administration's "lust" for Middle Eastern oil and the American public's "addiction" to debt, but those topics are not at issue here.) Here is what the author says is our religious problem:

The excesses of fundamentalism . . . are American and Is-
raeli, as well as the all-too-obvious depredations of radical
Islam. The rapture, end-times, and Armageddon hucksters
in the United States rank with any Shiite ayatollahs, and the
last two presidential elections mark the transformation of
the GOP into the first religious party in U.S. history.[23]

To start with, that paragraph is full of outright errors. The "first
religious party"? American history is filled with religious parties,
focused on various issues such as abolition and prohibition; more
than a few are active today, concerned especially with abortion;
and the Republican Party is scarcely composed only of believers,
let alone Christians of any particular denomination.

But, leaving that aside, who are the theocrats Phillips identifies
and accuses of putting the Constitution at risk? For one, that
ever-ready target of liberal smears, George W. Bush: "an elected
leader who believes himself in some way to speak for God," and
who leads the effort to implement "domestic and international
political agendas that seem to be driven by religious motivations
and biblical worldviews."[24] Besides President Bush, others cited
are the reverends Tim LaHaye, Pat Robertson, D. James Kennedy, and Jerry Falwell (the section of Phillips's book devoted to
theocracy is titled "Too Many Preachers"), psychologist James
Dobson, pretty much the entire Southern Baptist Convention,
and assorted members of Congress, typically from the South and
the West. And the Mormons. And the Seventh-Day Adventists.
But not Catholics, whom Phillips considers to be in rapid decline.
The Church, he says, no longer has much influence over its members, and they in turn have no influence over politics.

He writes:

In some ways the Emerging Republican Majority is becoming the Emerging Republican Theocracy, although that
might still be kept from fuller fruition. More broadly, suffice
it to say that the nation's most troublesome circumstances
owe much to the fealty of an erring Republican majority to
its most important constituencies.[25]

When he comes to his bill of particulars, there is nothing about
enforced worship or contributions to any church. Instead, his
"theocracy" amounts to positions against embryonic stem cell research and the starving of Terry Schiavo, and in support of Israel.
Jean Calvin would not be very impressed.

By the way, not one of the conservative Christian authors Phillips targets (LaHaye, Robertson, Kennedy, Falwell, and Dobson)
had a book on the best-seller list at the time the liberal books
mentioned above seemed to dominate. Each of these allegedly
theocratic authors has had best-selling books in the past and no
doubt will again (LaHaye especially), but there will have to be
one whopping Reformation of the best-seller lists for conservative Christian titles to demonstrate the kind of dominion, shall
we say, that the above-listed liberal books enjoyed. Indeed, looking at just the "religion & spirituality" category's top sellers at
Amazon in 2006, fifteen of the top twenty-five were liberal or un-
orthodox interpretations of Christianity. Only one, *The Purpose-
Driven Life* by Rick Warren, came from the "conservative,"
mega-church Christianity, which Phillips asserts is a threat to
America's survival. And Pastor Warren has kept himself out of
the political fray.

What is perhaps most curious is that, except for President
Bush, Phillips makes no direct accusation of theocracy against

any of those whose names he drops. Their guilt is established by association and innuendo.

Another Phillips, John McCandlish Phillips, longtime reporter for the *New York Times*, touched upon this problem of innuendo—which is to say, smear—in an article published in the *Washington Post* in May 2005, nearly a year before the other Phillips published *American Theocracy*. His article, "When Columnists Cry 'Jihad,'" [26] concluded that in fifty years of reporting, he had never encountered anything quite like the "fear and loathing" being served up in major newspapers on the subject of conservative Christians.* He cites in particular two of his former colleagues. In March 2005, Maureen Dowd began a column:

> Oh my God, we really are in a theocracy.
>
> Are the Republicans so obsessed with maintaining control over all branches of government, and are the Democrats so emasculated about not having any power, that they are willing to turn the nation into a wholly owned subsidiary of the church? . . .
>
> As the Bush White House desperately maneuvers in Iraq to prevent the new government from being run according to the dictates of religious fundamentalists, it desperately maneuvers here to pander to religious fundamentalists who want to dictate how the government should be run. [27]

---

*John Phillips is himself a Christian, and knows firsthand that religion may be counted as a disqualification in a reporter by his secular-minded colleagues. He is justly proud of a profile of him co-authored by two of the *Times*'s legendary figures, A. M. Rosenthal and Arthur Gelb, in which they stated: ". . . if having a Bible on his desk has been of any help to Phillips, the *Times* might well be advised to form a Gideon society of its own for the benefit of other reporters."

Three days later Frank Rich, whom John Phillips described as "an often acute, broadly knowledgeable and witty cultural observer," wrote:

> As Congress and the president scurried to play God in the lives of Terri Schiavo and her family last weekend, ABC kicked off Holy Week with its perennial ritual: a rebroadcast of the 1956 Hollywood blockbuster, *The Ten Commandments*.
>
> . . . this year the lovable old war horse has a relevance that transcends camp. At a time when government, culture, science, medicine and the rule of law are all under threat from an emboldened religious minority out to remake America according to its dogma, the half-forgotten show business history of *The Ten Commandments* provides a telling back story.[28]

Rich went so far as to declare that Bush and Company are engaged in a "full-scale jihad," which, with other examples he cites, led John Phillips to reflect that America's Founders "did not give us a nation frightened by the apparition of the Deity lurking about in our most central places." He emphasizes that on the very day the Founders adopted the First Amendment to the Constitution, they also passed a resolution asking President Washington to proclaim a day of thanksgiving to God.

Theocrats, Theocons, and Cons

It seems clear that Kevin Phillips did not speak with any of those often labeled as theocrats or theocons. I, however, did.

I asked for interviews with a number of Christian leaders (to my

knowledge, no Jews have ever been associated with theocracy—
not in America anyway—and are not subjects in *American Theocracy*, Phillips's sideswipe of Israel notwithstanding), and some
requests were declined. The subject of theocracy understandably
sets teeth on edge among some leading Christian personalities.
Choosing whom to speak to based upon *American Theocracy* was
something of a fishing expedition in any case, since, as I say, Phillips never actually names individual theocrats.

Of course, Phillips certainly indicates that Bush is a theocrat,
but I did not attempt to interview the president of the United
States for this book.

I began instead by discussing theocracy with the Rev. Christo
pher J. Ortiz, Director of Communications for the Chalcedon
(kal-SEE-dun) Foundation, a group more often associated with
theocracy than any other (and very much the target of Randall
Balmer's *Thy Kingdom Come*, mentioned above).

Consider how the folks at the Foundation describe their belief
in their own words:[29]

> The great problem with modern politics is that it is used as
> an instrument of social change. We at Chalcedon passion-
> ately oppose this. The role of the state is in essence to defend
> and protect, in the words of the early American Republic,
> life, liberty, and property. . . .
>
> [The State's] role is not to make men virtuous; we have a
> name for civil governments that attempt to create a virtuous
> society: totalitarian. Biblically, the role of the state is to sup-
> press external evil: murder, theft, rape, and so forth. Its role
> is not to redistribute wealth, furnish medical care, or educate
> its citizens' children.

We do believe that the state one day will be Christian, *but this in no way implies that the role of the state is to Christianize its citizens. The Christian state is highly decentralized (localized).* Our objective, therefore, in supporting Christian political involvement is to scale down the massive state in Western democracies, reducing it to its Biblical limits. *We do not believe in political salvation of any kind.* [Italicized emphases added.]

To be sure, this is strong stuff. And "theocracy" is indeed the word Chalcedon uses to describe its aim. But is it theocracy of the sort that so alarms Kevin Phillips? When I asked Dr. Ortiz whether there was any sense in which his beliefs about religion, politics, society, and law supported an American theocracy, his answer was clear:[30]

Not as Phillips defines it. I believe in theocracy, but not a *nationalist theocracy* which equates to a religious takeover of the present American governmental apparatus. Phillips, like other critics, confuses "theocracy" (i.e., the rule of God) with "ecclesiocracy" (i.e., the rule of the church, or a select religious elite). Biblical theocracy is what [Chalcedon founder R. J.] Rushdoony defined as a "radical libertarianism."

Dr. Ortiz added: "What you must keep in mind is that the theocratic vision of Christian Reconstruction would not be established for a very long time (some say thousands of years)."

I then assayed a theological tangent, asking Dr. Ortiz if the Creator made us free. His answer—kindly indulging the author—is instructive:

The whole concept of western liberty derives from Christendom. Yes, God made us desirous to be free. However, absolute freedom is a myth. Nobody is free to do WHATEVER they want. Law and liberty complement each other.

What must be remembered is that the Religious Right—which I do not endorse—has utilized the democratic process to achieve their present influence. Secularists can't whine that we're facing the death of democracy any more than a democratically controlled government equates to the end of Christianity in America. Both sides are guilty of sensationalism and exaggeration.

I next sought out Father Richard John Neuhaus, whom I have known since I was literary editor of *National Review* and he the magazine's religion editor. When we first met, in 1989, he was Pastor Neuhaus, a Lutheran, but a year later he became a Catholic and entered the priesthood. (He had been a man of the Left earlier in his life, and had been friends with—and had marched with—the Rev. Martin Luther King Jr.) Fr. Neuhaus is also the founder of *First Things: The Journal of Religion, Culture, and Public Life*, and he is probably most famous for having written a book about the increasing banishment of faith from civic life, the title of which has entered the nation's political discourse: *The Naked Public Square*. Fr. Neuhaus and I had lunch recently at a restaurant near the office of *First Things*.

I asked him for his reaction to Damon Linker's *The Theocons*, but he had yet to read it. He was, however, fully aware of the book, since it attacks him, since Linker had previously been an editor of *First Things*, and since a shortened version of the book had appeared a few months before in *The New Republic*. When

Linker told Fr. Neuhaus in 2005 that he wanted to write a book about *First Things*, Neuhaus volunteered complete, even joyful cooperation. However, he was frank with his young friend, suggesting that a book about his time at the magazine might not be of much interest to publishers. Fr. Neuhaus was accordingly surprised when Linker received a contract and an impressive cash incentive to do the book that became *The Theocons*. He was also surprised when Linker balked at showing him the proposal that had secured the deal. This was, Fr. Neuhaus would later write, "the first indication that he had agreed to write what in the publishing business is known as an 'attack book.' . . ."[31]

As to what Fr. Neuhaus actually believes, he and a group of likeminded Catholics and Evangelicals (the twenty-eight signatories of "That They May Have Life" include Protestant authors Rick Warren and Joni Eareckson Tada and Catholic authors Avery Cardinal Dulles and George Weigel) stated plainly their point of view:

> It is not the case that we wish to "impose" our moral convictions on our fellow citizens or, as some recklessly charge, to establish a "theocracy." Our intention is not to impose but to propose, educate, and persuade, in the hope that, through free deliberation and decision, our society will be turned toward a more consistent respect for the inestimable gift that is human life.[32]

It is hard to comprehend why Linker and Phillips would find such a statement frightening or objectionable. You couldn't ask for a clearer refutation of the "theocrat" charge. Indeed, the only plausible repudiation of their position would be the assertion that these distinguished Christians are lying, and I leave it to the reader to judge the plausibility of that.

At our lunch I asked Fr. Neuhaus about Linker's and Phillips's charges that a cabal of theocrats is out to undermine the Constitution. He shrugged and explained that some of his critics' alarm arose from a series of articles in *First Things* about the abortion issue that led to discussion of the American "regime" and the possibility of revolution against the reigning orthodoxy (or heterodoxy, depending upon one's perspective).

" 'Revolution' is a strong word," I said.

"It is," Fr. Neuhaus agreed. "But this nation is founded upon the premise that there are times when governments lose their legitimacy and that when that happens—and we're nowhere near that point in the United States—we have not only the right but also the responsibility to change that government."

In the end, none of those so often cited as theocrats actually endorses any sort of theocracy or any sort of polity that would put at risk anything we consider essentially American. None of the sources cited by Phillips in making his arguments actually discusses theocracy at all, and none of those he seems to suggest are theocrats actually believes there is or ought to be a theocratic movement of consequence in the United States today or in the foreseeable future. Thus it seems safe to conclude that, when he compares evangelical or fundamentalist leaders to Iranian mullahs and other genuine theocrats, Phillips has smeared American Christians. And given that that those real theocrats—the ones in Iran and elsewhere—have regularly called for the murder of Christians and Jews, the smear seems particularly egregious.

The ever insightful Mark Steyn had a nice take on Linker's thesis that Fr. Neuhaus and others have engaged in, to use Linker's words, a "stealth campaign" (an odd description for a crusade carried out so publicly) to create a future "in which American politics and culture have been systematically purged of secularism," especially with regard to sexual ethics. Steyn comments with irony:

> [S]o far the conspiracy seems to be going swimmingly, with the Supreme Court claiming to have discovered a constitutional right to sodomy and its fellow jurists in Massachusetts having legalized gay marriage. That's exactly the kind of cunning distraction you'd expect these theocons to come up with to throw the rest of us off the scent.[33]

As is so often the case with smears, there is a powerful amount of hypocrisy involved in accusations of American right-wing theocracy. The Left expresses deep concern about the authority and influence of, as Kevin Phillips puts it, too many preachers—all those Reverends: LaHaye, Falwell, Robertson, and the rest; all the theocons or theocrats or Christocrats, the Christian Nationalists or Christianists or . . . simply Christians. But when the subject is progressive causes and the efforts of those who champion them, then there is silence about faith. When have liberals complained about the *Reverend* Jesse Jackson or the *Reverend* Al Sharpton? Or, dare I say, of Fr. Neuhaus's old friend, the *Reverend* Martin Luther King Jr.?

And now a final word about the most enduring smear of them all: anti-Semitism.

Old Whine in New Battles

Writing at the Salon.com Web site, movie critic Neal Gabler saw the 2006 DUI arrest of actor-director Mel Gibson, during which

Gibson went into an anti-Semitic tirade ("[Expletive] Jews....
The Jews are responsible for all the wars in the world"), as saying
something ominous not only about Gibson but also about American conservatism, American Christianity, and indeed about
America itself in the Bush era:

> Mel Gibson . . . does not operate within that elevated envi-
> ronment, because America itself has changed—one might
> even say has been radicalized—since the election of George
> Bush. The merger of evangelical Christianity, which has
> long had a tinge of racism and anti-Semitism, with right-
> wing Republicanism has had many effects on American cul-
> ture and politics, but perhaps the foremost among them is
> that it has legitimized attitudes that were previously consid-
> ered illegitimate by the custodians of the social order. Mel
> Gibson has not only been the beneficiary of that change; he
> has courted those who effected it—those for whom extrem-
> ism in the defense of their version of liberty is no vice.[34]

This would seem to suggest that Gibson's rant to the sheriff's
deputies who pulled him over in Malibu was considered by
many—perhaps most—Americans as completely understandable;
that conservative Christians (Gabler is explicit about Christianity
and more implicitly evokes conservatism by quoting the 1964 acceptance speech of Barry Goldwater) had simply brushed off the
incident as meaningless, or had actually endorsed it; and that, in
fact, conservative Christians are racist and anti-Semitic.

But researching the public reaction to Gibson's anti-Semitic
comments reveals no such endorsement. Indeed nearly all conservative and Christian commentators were united in condemnation
of Gibson's remarks. Why then the assumption that the reaction

would be indulgent? Dennis Prager, who is conservative and Jewish, offers an explanation:

> The liberal world fears—and much of it loathes—fundamentalist Christians. . . .
>
> This is as true of most Jewish liberals—even though conservative Christians are Israel's and the Jews' most loyal supporters. . . ."[35]

As Prager points out, the Gibson story dominated headlines around the country even though on the same day a Muslim man, Naveed Haq, had shot up a Seattle Jewish center, killing one and wounding five.

> The antipathy toward Christian fundamentalists and conservatives is why Mel Gibson's anti-Semitic statements trouble the Left more than Naveed Haq and the genocidal anti-Semitism permeating the Muslim world. And what is it about those Christians that most disturbs the Left? That they talk in terms of good and evil and believe the former must fight the latter, precisely the area of the Left's greatest weakness.[36]

Evangelical author and radio host Hugh Hewitt called Gibson's outburst "repulsive," and a story in the *Washington Post* confirmed that this was the attitude of most Christian leaders. Despite the story's headline, "Evangelical Clergy on Mel Gibson: Judging Not," the article makes clear that no "tinge" of anti-Semitism, to reprise Gabler's word choice, was evident in evangelical reaction to Gibson's arrest.

Gibson's drunken remarks about "[expletive] Jews" being responsible for "all the wars in the world," which the actor made to a Los Angeles sheriff's deputy who pulled him over on July 28, were "hurtful and unfortunate" (James C. Dobson), "reprehensible . . . shameful" (the Rev. James Merritt) and "cause for concern" (the Rev. Ted Haggard).[37]

Indeed, the article's headline is actually a reference to Gibson's film, *The Passion of the Christ*, and not to his arrest. The Christian leaders interviewed for the article were unwilling to recant their earlier endorsement of that film on the basis of Gibson's later arrest. Dr. Haggard, for instance, agreed that Gibson's comments probably reflected the actor-director's true thoughts in some sense but added that "high quality films, books and sermons are made, written and preached by severely imperfect people. The film stands on its own."

The backstory to Gibson's outburst is that while he was making *The Passion of the Christ*, various Jewish organizations and commentators—most prominently the Anti-Defamation League—had kept up relentless pressure for nearly a year to get him to alter the script. Specifically, they wanted him to soften the scenes involving the high priest, Caiaphas, and the Jewish crowd. As a Q&A on the ADL's Web site put it:

As anti-Semitism increases around the globe, many are using the age-old deicide charge to legitimize and foment hatred against Jews. Our concerns have already become an excuse for an outpouring of anti-Semitism. Since going public with our concerns about the film, ADL and other Jewish organizations have been flooded with hate-filled e-mails, letters and phone calls.[38]

Gibson insisted that those scenes were not motivated by anti-Semitism—they were simply faithful to the Bible—and he refused to alter them. In the event, there were no incidents of violence against Jews attributable to the film. But of course commentators were quick to read Gibson's rant back into the film. One blogger wrote:

> I am trying to imagine Mel Gibson in his best "they'll never take our freedom" voice. If it weren't for the anti-Semitic comments then I would actually find this funny. But it just goes to show the real bias behind that movie.[39]

Gibson himself offered a different explanation: that the barrage of Jewish criticism of his film had left a simmering resentment.[40]

In any case, the Gibson story broke with full force on July 28, 2006, and by August 1 he had issued a carefully worded apology, along with the promise that he was entering an alcoholism recovery program. It's hard not to be at least a little cynical about that, given the number of celebrities who flee to rehab whenever they have acted either foolishly or criminally, but he did apologize: thoroughly and quickly. But that didn't stop the ADL from issuing a response that read in part: "This is the apology we had sought and requested. We are glad that Mel Gibson has finally owned up to the fact that he made anti-Semitic remarks. . . ."

Finally? It took three days.

Meanwhile, it was left to the inimitable Bill Maher to round the incident out with a stunning smear of Christianity:

When Mel's id is released, it's about the Jews f—ing everything up, just like it was with Hitler. Except Mel Gibson,
when his id is in check, I believe, really knows how wrong
that is, and how stupid. He, I believe, at least fights with
himself about this.

But he'll never win as long as he's so religious, because, I
hate to tell you, the disease isn't alcoholism, the disease is
religion.[41]

So why does the Left seem to attack religion so frequently and
with such passion? Much as Dennis Prager suggested, simply because the Left despises religion and so attacks the faithful: Protestant, Catholic, and Jew. Muslims are usually spared, because by
some perverse logic their "foreignness" keeps them sheltered be-
neath the aegis of multiculturalism.

Faith as Pathology

A prime example of what Prager is talking about is one of the
books listed at the start of this chapter: *Breaking the Spell: Religion
as Natural Phenomenon* by Daniel C. Dennett. Prof. Dennett, of
Tufts University, makes much the same argument about religious
belief that the Berkeley study we considered in Chapter 2 made
about conservatism: that it is actually an illness, for which a cure
must be found.

Dennett is a self-described "Darwinian fundamentalist" and a
"bright," by which he means *atheist*. He tells of his desire, "mod-
eled on the highly successful hijacking of the ordinary word 'gay'
by homosexuals," to coin a positive term for nonbelievers, and

then he archly explains that even if his term catches on, that doesn't mean that religious people have to be "dims":

> Those who are not gays are not necessarily glum; they're *straight*. Those who are not brights are not necessarily dim. They might like to choose a name for themselves. Since, unlike us brights, they believe in the supernatural, perhaps they would like to call themselves *supers*. It's a nice word with positive connotations, like *gay* and *bright* and *straight*.[42]

Religious people cannot begrudge Dr. Dennett his materialist view of life—until, that is, he employs his own irreligion to justify the claim that faith is an illness. Because Dr. Dennett is convinced there is no such thing as God, it must follow that those who believe are victims of a delusion—whether it is manifest as a cargo cult or as Christianity, though the size and power of the latter clearly marks it as the most pathological of all.

To Dennett, the worst thing about religion is that parents who are believers claim the right to pass their beliefs on to their children:

> On the one hand, many declare, there is the sacred and inviolable right to life: every unborn child has a right to life, and no prospective parent has the right to terminate a pregnancy (except maybe if the mother's life is itself in jeopardy). On the other hand, many of the same people declare that, once born, the child loses its right not to be indoctrinated or brainwashed or otherwise psychologically abused by those parents, who have the right to raise the child with any upbringing they choose, short of physical torture. Let us spread

the value of freedom throughout the world—but not to children, apparently. No child has a right to freedom from indoctrination. Shouldn't we change that? What, and let *outsiders* have a say in how I raise *my kids*? (Now do you feel the adrenaline rush?)[13]

I raise the subject of Dennett here mainly to be able to quote David B. Hart's blistering review of *Breaking the Spell* from Fr. Neuhaus's magazine, *First Things*, and I do so for two reasons: first, because it deals so powerfully with Dennett's smear of faith and the way he cloaks the smear with scientific jargon; and, second, because it's a reminder that criticizing—even if the criticism is harsh—is not smearing.

All Dennett knows is that something he dreads haunts the world, something intolerant and violent and irrational, and he wants to conjure it away. This, of course, raises the ... question of how, in the wake of the twentieth century, the committed secularist dare wax either sanctimonious toward faith or sanguine toward secular reason, but Dennett is not one to pause before doubts of that sort. He is certain there is some single immense thing out there called religion, and that by its very nature it endangers us all and ought as a whole to be abolished. This being so, it is probably less important to him that his argument be good than that, for purely persuasive purposes, it appear to be grounded in irrefutable science—which it can never be.[44]

V

SMEARING ENTREPRENEURS

[B]ecause communism and even socialism have been thoroughly discredited, I consider the threat from the laissez-faire side more potent today than the threat from totalitarian ideologies.

—*Billionaire George Soros, writing in the* Atlantic Monthly[1]

THE RECENT PROPOSAL BY THE EUROPEAN Union to cap the salaries of soccer players (footballers, as they would say) may be a portent of things to come in America.[2] We frequently hear complaints about the salaries of professional athletes and corporate executives and about the profits made by various industries, from oil companies to fast-food chains. When Hollywood goes looking for a villain, the capitalist is the likely bad guy, and our schools are generally doing nothing to enhance the image of business and entrepreneurship. As British journalist James Bartholomew wrote:

They teach that capitalists destroy rainforests, insidiously control American foreign policy and spread human vices of greed and selfishness. Anti-capitalism is now the subtext of history and geography lessons, as well as politics, economics and sociology. Capitalism is said to have given rise to slavery. The state is depicted as a hero that has tempered the cruelty of the beast with laws, regulations and interventions.[3]

Professor Larry E. Ribstein, in his scholarly paper "Wall Street and Vine: Hollywood's View of Business,"[4] gives dozens of examples from the movies. Some of these are acknowledged fiction; others, like *Erin Brockovich*, are, according to their publicity, "based on true events"—but only as far as it suits the filmmakers' purposes. In the case of the real-life Erin Brockovich, Ribstein points out, there is no evidence that the suspect chemical caused the harm that sent Brockovich on her crusade.

But there are plenty of other examples:

Many other films portray business as the enemy of the people. Examples include *A Civil Action* (1998), in which sympathetic star John Travolta handles a case in which an unusual number of childhood leukemia cases seem to be associated with a water supply that may be contaminated by something [W. R.] Grace dumps in it; *The Insider* (1999), in which sympathetic star Russell Crowe exposes his tobacco company employer for hiding evidence that cigarettes hurt people; *The China Syndrome* (1979), in which sympathetic Jack Lemmon plays a company insider who, along with a television reporter played by sympathetic star Jane Fonda, exposes a cover-up of safety problems in a nuclear power plant; *Silkwood* (1983), in which Karen Silkwood, portrayed by the sympathetic Meryl Streep, may or may not have been killed for uncovering dangerous practices at a nuclear power plant.

The pervasiveness of this theme in films is indicated by the sometimes odd and incidental ways in which it appears. For example: the evil drug company in *Mission Impossible II* (2000) creates a virus in order to sell the cure. *The Fugitive* (1993) added to the television series on which it was based the spin that the one-armed man who killed the fugitive's wife worked for a drug company that sought to cover forged test results in pursuit of enormous profits. The protagonist in *Fight Club* (1999) struck out against, among other things, the corporate irresponsibility he saw in his job handling recalls for an automobile company.[5]

The Media Research Center's Business & Media Institute (BMI) studied the movies that received the top Academy Award nominations in 2006 (that is, the nominations for Best Picture, Director, Actor, Actress, Supporting Actor, and Supporting Actress). It found that

> half of the movies earning top Oscar nominations (8 of 16) portrayed businessmen in either primary or secondary roles committing crimes. The list of their crimes was staggering—drug use, drug smuggling, prostitution, corruption, assault, attempted murder, murder and genocide.
>
> One of the characters in *The Constant Gardener* tried to defend how a business had used poor Africans as guinea pigs for a new drug. "We're not killing people who wouldn't be dead otherwise," he claimed.
>
> That was one of three films that marshaled direct assaults against entire industries: coal mining (*North Country*); oil (*Syriana*); and pharmaceuticals (*The Constant Gardener*). The

first two, along with *Good Night, and Good Luck*, were decidedly liberal and/or anti-business propaganda pictures sponsored by eBay billionaire Jeff Skoll.

Hollywood directors hid behind claims that these movies reflected reality. All three of the Skoll productions were purportedly based on history. Half of the top Oscar nominees made similar claims or were at least "inspired by actual events."[6]

Quite simply, nothing rankles the elites more than the free market, because the market is the place where millions upon millions of ordinary (and extraordinary) people meet to make decisions about quality, quantity, and price—often without reference to what the elites' opinions happen to be. That free-market capitalism also happens to have been—and continues to be—the greatest force for prosperity for the mass of mankind, which doesn't help the mood of those who are convinced that all businessmen care about is their own interests and that those interests must be inimical to the interests of the poor. Of course those same critics have never been able to explain why under the aegis of the free market prices fall—how the average amount of wealth spent in the developed world on, for instance, food has plummeted, and why under communism there were daily lines for bread. Why is it we never see movies about that?

Limousine Liberalism

The title of any number of Internet articles and postings is "Hollywood Hates America," which is certainly hyperbole: plenty of people who make movies and TV shows do love their country.

But there is also no doubt that filmmakers (much like their cousins in the news media) are by and large left of center politically, and that their leftism often shows itself—artfully of course—in the characters portrayed as villains and in the presentation (or misrepresentation) of facts.

Prof. Ribstein conjectures that American films' "negative view of business" stems from the filmmakers' "resentment of capitalists' constraints on their artistic vision."[7] It is not, of course, the epochal conflict of "capital" versus "labor," since in this case labor consists mainly of millionaire directors and producers and, of course, "the talent," the actors and actresses who in many cases are pulling down seven-figure salaries.

Beginning fairly early in the twentieth century, Hollywood had a very serious flirtation with radicalism, including communism. And the film colony's soft spot for the Left included not just the domestic Left but even some of the last century's more despotic regimes. A few years ago, Kenneth Lloyd Billingsley, writing in *Reason* magazine, wrote a deadpan review of *Total Eclipse*, a powerful Stephen Spielberg film about the 1939 Nazi-Soviet Pact, starring many of Hollywood's leading actors. After seven paragraphs recounting the film's high points in detail, Billingsley writes:

> Never heard of *Total Eclipse*? It hasn't been produced or even written. In all likelihood, such a film has never even been contemplated, at least in Hollywood. Indeed, in the decade since the Berlin Wall fell, or even the decade before that, no Hollywood film has addressed the actual history of communism, the agony of the millions whose lives were poisoned by it, and the century of international deceit that obscured com-

munist reality. The simple but startling truth is that the major conflict of our time, democracy versus Marxist-Leninist totalitarianism—what *The New York Times* recently called "the holy war of the 20th century"—is almost entirely missing from American cinema. It is as though since 1945, Hollywood had produced little or nothing about the victory of the Allies and the crimes of National Socialism. This void is all the stranger since the major conflict of our time would seem to be a natural draw for Hollywood.[8]

Hollywood has not made *Total Eclipse*, or any film like it, because producers and directors simply find it more convenient to attack the soldiers and patriots who defend America, the people who pray for America, and the men and women who create and sustain the American economy. And, as Saint Paul might put it, in the eyes of Tinseltown, the slimiest of these is the businessman.

In Oliver Stone's Oscar-winning drama *Wall Street*, antihero Gordon Gekko famously proclaims that greed is good. "Greed is right," he says. "Greed works. Greed clarifies." (Once during a panel discussion, Stone was challenged about his facts. He responded: "Even if I am totally wrong . . . I am still right. . . . I am essentially right because I am depicting the Evil with a capital E."[9]) In a less famous but utterly revealing speech, Gekko says:

The richest one percent of this country owns half our country's wealth, five trillion dollars. One third of that comes from hard work, two thirds comes from inheritance, interest on interest accumulating to widows and idiot sons and what I do, stock and real estate speculation. It's bullshit. You got ninety percent of the American public out there with little or no net worth. I create nothing. I own. We make the rules, pal. The news, war, peace, famine, upheaval, the price per paper clip. We pick that rabbit out of the hat while everybody sits out there wondering how the hell we did it. Now you're not naive enough to think we're living in a democracy, are you buddy? It's the free market.[10]

As in movies, so also on TV: a thorough study of hundreds of television programs shows that "businessmen are more than three times as likely to be criminals [as] are members of other occupations."[11]

The Media Research Center's Business & Media Institute found that "TV dramas [are] overwhelmingly negative toward business by 4 to 1. Businessmen were portrayed as villains, not heroes. According to TV dramas, you were 21 times more likely to be kidnapped or murdered at the hands of a businessman than by the mob."[12]

To return to Prof. Ribstein's view of Hollywood's portrayal of business, he asserts that the film industry isn't so much against capitalism as it is against capitalists. I'm uncertain this is a distinction with meaning. He—and writer Phillip Lopate, whom he quotes—believe that the bias in films comes from the creative filmmaker's frustration at sometimes having to modify his vision to suit the financial backers of the film. No doubt, but it is those moneymen who are taking the risk. And despite this, as Ribstein acknowledges, "the constraints of [the financier's risk-taking] are too weak to prevent artists from expressing their resentment" against the very system that allows them to thrive. If you were putting up money for an Oliver Stone film, you probably wouldn't care what the director's biases are as long as you were convinced his movies would make money. Indeed, you'd depend upon those biases, since they seem to be keys to Stone's success. But Lopate's notion that it's not capitalism itself that is being attacked in some films is almost perverse. The words of Gordon Gekko are an obvious parody of the great classical economist Adam Smith, which is to say they are an attack on the system of capitalism itself.

Besides, very little evidence has been cited to support the contention that filmmakers and their producers don't really oppose the system, just the rapacious moneygrubbers who themselves may be said to denigrate the spirit of capitalism. If Hollywood were really not against capitalism, we might expect to see the odd film about a good businessman—about the risks and rewards of starting and running an enterprise; a film that would actually reflect the reality that honest men and women succeed and fail in a moral environment in which competitive market forces determine the outcome. But the so-called progressive vision won't allow this. Thus when a time-traveling Star Fleet Captain Jean-Luc Picard describes the future to somebody, he says that "the economics of the 24th century are different—people are no longer motivated by money, but rather by the good of mankind."[13]

This is the sort of dialogue that passes for forward thinking, but it is actually a description—intended or not—of a statist approach to economics that simply ignores the failures of socialism, communism, and fascism, in which "the good of mankind" rather than individual freedom was seen as the engine of a vibrant and just economy. The consequences, as we now know, were catastrophic.

To say that the media in general—and not just the movies specifically—are anticapitalist is an understatement. No organization has done more than the Washington, D.C.–based Media Research Center to document the bias against business, as it did in its 2002 survey, "A Summer of Skewed News: The Liberal Tilt in TV's Economic Reporting." This report focuses especially on the network news attacks on the free market and entrepreneurs.[14] The report stated:

> The big story at the beginning of the summer was the fiscal health of corporate America. As major companies such as Enron, Global Crossing and WorldCom became embroiled in accounting scandals, network reporters seemed to have just one suggestion: more government regulations. If the President refused to embrace new rules, journalists suggested, it wasn't because he was a principled conservative, but a slave to big business.

The report's author, MRC Director of Media Analysis Rich Noyes, offered some specifics:

- CNN's Aaron Brown: "This is a President who has made no bones about the fact that he is not a great fan of regulation, he talks about cooperation, not regulation. Does he have a credibility problem?"
- CBS's Wyatt Andrews: "[Bush is the] President who, for most of his term, has been 'partner-in-chief' with big business."
- CBS's John Roberts: "While people are split over whether Mr. Bush is more interested in protecting large corporations or ordinary Americans, there is no question they feel his staff comes down on the side of corporations."

The corporate scandals during the period covered in the report made inquiries by the press into corporate governance entirely appropriate. The trouble is, commentary on the scandals seemed

to diminish the institution of the free market as much as it criticized the managers of the failed companies. It's the system, liberal
critics insist, not the men, and the only effective reform will involve government regulation, not individual responsibility.

Super-Sized Alarmists

The liberal, activist New York City Council, which has over the
years passed a series of increasingly strict bans on smoking, decided in December 2006 to take on a different menace: trans fats,
the cholesterol-containing substances found especially in "fast
food." Critics of the ban claim that this is an extreme example of
"nanny-state" politics—of an elite of liberal politicians deciding
that we, the people, cannot be left to decide for ourselves what is
good to eat.

For the purposes of this book, the question is: Do the ban and
the rhetoric that accompanied it constitute a smear on those
whom the Council proposes to help? Was the Council suggesting
that the city's poor cannot be left to make eating decisions on
their own? (It's unlikely the ban was really aimed at the wealthy
denizens of the city's tonier restaurants, which may offer plenty of
cholesterol, but not in the form of the "artificial trans fats" specifically banned by the City Council.)

Some of the rhetoric occasioned by the vote amounted to
super-sized smears. We might expect it from Howard Stern:
"Ring Dings have 2 grams [of trans fats], Denny's Carrot Cake
has 3 grams . . . if this stuff was being sold by a terrorist nation,
they would all be under arrest, we would be bombing them right
now for killing us." [15]

But here is the respected *New York Times* columnist Nicholas

Kristof: "The problem is that most of those Girl Scout Cookies have trans fatty acids. Those are the worst kind of fat, killing far more Americans than Al Qaeda manages to."[16]

And New York city councilman Peter Vallone Jr. offered this judicious statement at the city Health Department hearings: "Trans fats kill babies!"[17]

Three years before the City Council action, two New York teenagers sued McDonald's because it had made them obese. One of their attorneys, John Banzhaf, said, "When we're suing on behalf of children, it's hard to argue that a 6, or 8 or 10-year-old child has to take full responsibility for their decisions when they're lured into McDonald's by the toys and the playground and happy meals and the birthday parties."[18] *Six-year-olds* are taking "full responsibility" over whether or not to eat at McDonald's? As for their parents, a spokesman points out that McDonald's has poster-sized charts on the walls listing the nutritional content of all its offerings.

It is unlikely that the City Council in the nation's most media-savvy city was not influenced at least in part by two recent media phenomena: Morgan Spurlock's movie *Super Size Me* (2004) and Eric Schlosser's book *Fast Food Nation: The Dark Side of the All-American Meal* (2001).

In Spurlock's film, he made himself the subject of an experiment to discover how consuming three fast-food meals a day at McDonald's restaurants for one month would affect his thirty-two-year-old body. He gained twenty-five pounds and his serum cholesterol count rose by sixty-two points. According to the film, there were other health complications, including liver damage. Sounds scary.

But novelist Chuck Klosterman, for whom Spurlock did an in-home screening of the film, is skeptical. He himself had done a similar experiment several years before Spurlock's—also at Mc-Donald's. He ate, he wrote in *Esquire* magazine, nothing but Chicken McNuggets for one week—granted, a much shorter time period for the experiment. "And you know what happened to me? Nothing. Nothing happened. I gained exactly one pound. My cholesterol and blood pressure actually went down"[19]—though he does write that he felt during that McNugget-eating week as though he were coated in petroleum jelly. Still, he raises an important point: conclusions derived from so limited an experiment—one man over one month or one week—simply do not constitute objective evidence of larger principles. Klosterman suggested the same to Spurlock, who acknowledged that a month of eating broccoli would probably have adverse effects as well. "But you know what? Nobody is telling you that broccoli is a meal. Mc-Donald's is trying to convince people that their stuff is a legitimate meal, and that you can have it every day."[20]

But is that what McDonald's is doing? No. The nation's largest restaurant chain is simply offering a product that consumers clearly want at a price those consumers can afford.

In an interview with Maria Bartiromo on the CNBC program *Special Report*, Spurlock tried to explain why McDonald's was subject to especial enmity in his movie:

> Well, I mean, the thing is—is I never really—the—the—you know, the film is not about McDonald's. McDonald's in the film is iconic of a problem. McDonald's is there because they are the one that is the largest, the one whose marketing practices are most insidious, the one who, you know, continues to branch out in more countries. . . . You know, so I picked them as—as a symbol of—of our lifestyle. . . . [21]

Spurlock chose McDonald's because of the near ubiquity of the chain across America and throughout the world. That ubiquity makes it an easy target, but Spurlock might just as well have attacked eating itself. Dr. Ruth Kava, director of nutrition at the American Council on Science and Health, notes that comparing the American diet in the 1970s with what we consumed in the 1990s reveals that on average we consumed an additional two hundred calories per day.

Since the '90s, the picture hasn't improved. Recently the Centers for Disease Control and Prevention (CDC) published the results of another survey summary—this one examining energy intake between 1971 and 2000 by adults between the ages of 20 and 74. Again, total reported calorie intake increased for both men and women. For men, the increase was on the order of about 170 calories and for women over 300 calories.[22]

This is clearly a serious matter with dire implications for the health of individuals who overindulge, but Dr. Kava's point is that the nationwide uptick in calorie intake is across the board and that to single out McDonald's is, as she puts it, "A Supersized Distortion." Put another way: folks who dine at every kind of restaurant and folks who eat only at home are overeating at the same pace as diners at McDonald's.

As for Spurlock's "experiment," it must be noted that whereas overeating for a person of average height and weight might be defined as taking in more than two thousand calories a day, Spurlock consumed five thousand calories a day during his McDonald's binge. And calories are calories. Had he consumed that amount eating "health food" rather than fast food, he'd likely have gained the same amount of weight.

And in the interview with Ms. Bartiromo, Spurlock admitted that he had, in fact, snacked between his McDonald's meals. When she pointed out to him that another documentarian, Soso Wiley, had done exactly what he did—eating three squares a day at McDonald's—and *lost* ten pounds, he insisted that the comparison wasn't fair. Ms. Wiley was actually exercising at the same time and eating less—notwithstanding that all her calories were coming from McDonald's. Spurlock said, "What are the two things no American does? Americans don't eat less and we don't exercise. You know, these—Of course you're going to lose weight if you eat less and exercise. That—Those go hand in hand. Welcome to America, where that doesn't happen."[23]

That seems a strange conclusion about a country in which diet and exercise books and videos are perennial best sellers. If what Spurlock means is that, given available options, many people choose to eat what they want and not to exercise, then he is simply describing the conditions of a free society. And if he thinks government ought to intervene to stop fast-food chains from serving what people want to eat, he needs to explain himself in terms of America's tradition of liberty, which probably is asking too much.

Ditto Eric Schlosser, whose *Fast Food Nation* is another broadside against fast food and free choice. He writes:

Elitists have always looked down at fast food, criticizing how it tastes and regarding it as another tacky manifestation of American popular culture. The aesthetics of fast food are of much less concern to me than its impact upon the lives of ordinary Americans, both as workers and consumers. Most of all, I am concerned about its impact on the nation's children. Fast food is heavily marketed to children and prepared by people who are barely older than children. This is an industry that both feeds and feeds off the young. . . . [T]he value meals, two-for-one deals, and free refills of soda give a distorted sense of how much fast food actually costs. The real price never appears on the menu.[24]

As one commentator describes the book:

Mr. Schlosser's sermonizing language betrays a shocking anti business bias and contempt for free market choices. The cover . . . includes a sinister subtitle, "The Dark Side of the All-American Meal." But a Whopper with fries and a Coke and their ingredients are neither moral nor immoral. They are not captains of their souls, nor masters of their fates. Human beings are.[25]

Schlosser's premise is that McDonald's, Burger King, and other fast-food restaurants manipulate patrons through advertising to consume what they would otherwise not consume. But, per Dr. Kava's comments above, Americans' food choices are pretty bad across the board. And the successful marketing and competition within the fast-food industry has brought down food prices and generally improved quality, in the sense of variety and flavor, in the food it serves, which now includes more healthy alternatives. These are now on fast-food menus not as a result of efforts by either Spurlock or Schlosser, but precisely because the corporations running the restaurants recognized that it is good business to provide more choices their customers will enjoy. Elite opinion will always assume it knows better than others what is right for those others, but—and this is not hyperbole—the elites are always wrong.

Schlosser concludes that we need more federal programs aimed at improving the health of American citizens and increasing the power of labor unions, which he sees as an effective counterbalance to the power of the corporations he believes exploit the credulity of consumers. Thomas DiLorenzo observes that "Schlosser reveals his true agenda in the book's epilogue, where he sings the praises of 'scientific socialists,' a term that Lenin used to boast of the alleged accomplishments of Soviet socialism. He lambastes capitalism in general and waxes eloquent about the alleged munificence of government intervention. . . ."[26]

Richard Linklater's film version of Schlosser's *Fast Food Nation* was shown to appreciative audiences at the Cannes Film Festival in France but was somewhat overshadowed by Al Gore's *An Inconvenient Truth* in a year when Cannes "went green." Meanwhile, "the McDonald's located directly across the street from the Palais des Festivals, where the movies were being shown, [did] brisk business" during the Festival.[27] But then, as another recent best seller about food has it, that's okay because *French Women Don't Get Fat*.

Green with Envy

It may not seem obvious at first why a discussion of the environment is appropriate in a chapter devoted to liberal attitudes about business, but it will, I hope, become clear that alarmism about the environment and smears of capitalism are intimately related. We certainly have reached a point at which that alarmism—about global warming especially—has led some on the Left to make extraordinary accusations against those who caution against making overly grand assertions about temperature data.

Writing in the *Boston Globe*, columnist Ellen Goodman recently asserted that the report of the United Nations' Intergovernmental Panel on Climate Change (IPCC) makes the fact of global warming "unequivocal," and therefore: "I would like to say we're at a point where global warming is impossible to deny. Let's just say that global warming deniers are now on a par with Holocaust deniers, though one denies the past and the other denies the present and future."[28]

Goodman is far from alone in spreading this outrageous smear. At this writing, Google indicates that it has about 359,000 entries for "global-warming deniers." That's up from 80,000 last October. Perhaps the most famous utterer of this smear is former vice president Al Gore, who believes that the question of global warming is no longer one of science: "This is being redefined as a choice between good and evil."[29]

In a more jocular vein, he said: "Fifteen per cent of the population believe the moon landing was actually staged in a movie lot in Arizona and somewhat fewer still believe the Earth is flat. I think they should all get together with the global warming deniers on a Saturday night and party."[30]

Over at CBS, Brian Montopoli, editor of CBS News's *Public Eye*, asked a colleague, *60 Minutes* correspondent Scott Pelley, why in his feature programs on global warming he did not include the views of global-warming skeptics. Pelley replied, "If I do an interview with Elie Wiesel, am I required as a journalist to find a Holocaust denier? . . . There comes a point in journalism where striving for balance becomes irresponsible."[31]

Now, many who caution against rushing headlong into policy

changes based on theories of global warming do not actually deny that there is warming. Even those who do question the warming data can hardly be said to compare to people who choose to ignore the documentary evidence of the extermination of European Jewry. For one thing, the future is by definition unknown, and any and all speculations about it are that—speculations, no matter how well informed. With regard to the present, data may be interpreted differently. Indeed, data are interpreted differently. Goodman's column confirms it. She writes that whereas only 23 percent of college-educated Republicans believe warming is due to human activity, 75 percent of college-educated Democrats believe that it is. Her conclusion is that Republicans are denying the truth, but why would that be the conclusion? Wouldn't it be just as sensible—and far less sinister—to suggest that Republicans are more cautious in taking costly actions that might not prove effective? Or that Democrats are too credulous of media reports about science? But Goodman is angry enough to smear the whole of the Republican Party and the Establishment it represents:

> This great divide comes from the science-be-damned-and-debunked attitude of the Bush administration and its favorite media outlets. The day of the report, Big Oil Senator James Inhofe of Oklahoma actually described it as "a shining example of the corruption of science for political gain." Speaking of corruption of science, the American Enterprise Institute, which has gotten $1.6 million over the years from ExxonMobil, offered $10,000 last summer to scientists who would counter the IPCC report.

Ignore for a moment the "Big Oil Senator" smear, and consider the claim about the researchers from the American Enterprise Institute (AEI). Goodman was referring to two men, scholars Kenneth Green and Steven Mansfield, who had recently been attacked in Britain's *The Guardian* by journalist Ian Sample. Sample's article, "Scientists Offered Cash to Dispute Climate Study," alleged that Green and Mansfield "offered . . . payments for articles that emphasize the shortcomings" of the UN report. Sample also characterized AEI as an "ExxonMobil-funded" "lobby group" with "close links to the Bush administration." He quotes Ben Stewart of Greenpeace, who says:

> The AEI is more than just a thinktank, it functions as the Bush administration's intellectual Cosa Nostra. They are White House surrogates in the last throes of their campaign of climate change denial. They lost on the science; they lost on the moral case for action. All they've got left is a suitcase full of cash.[32]

As Green and Hayward reported in *The Weekly Standard*, Sample "spoke to one of us for five minutes . . . but he clearly was not interested in learning the full story." And what was that story? Simply that AEI, which does no lobbying, had indeed offered payment for papers—but from a wide range of scientists, including proponents of the UN climate panel's conclusions. More than this:

> It is possible to accept the general consensus about the existence of global warming while having valid questions about the extent of warming, the consequences of warming, and the appropriate responses. In particular, one can remain a *policy* skeptic, which is what we are today, along with nearly all economists.[33]

AEI commissioned essays from a range of experts about climate change and its implications with no intention of ignoring the diversity of opinions, and it offered payment for the 7,500 to 10,000-word essays—and the review of "thousands of pages of material"—to *everyone* it approached, which is standard practice in the world of think tanks.

As to policy implications, *Newsweek* columnist Robert Samuelson soberly noted in the *Washington Post*:

> Don't be fooled. The dirty secret about global warming is this: We have no solution. About 80 percent of the world's energy comes from fossil fuels (coal, oil, natural gas), the main sources of man-made greenhouse gases. Energy use sustains economic growth, which—in all modern societies—buttresses political and social stability. Until we can replace fossil fuels or find practical ways to capture their emissions, governments will not sanction the deep energy cuts that would truly affect global warming.[34]

Which is why during the Clinton administration the Senate of the United States passed a "sense of the Senate resolution" rejecting the Kyoto Protocol, which would have imposed draconian measures on the world economy, by a vote of 95–0—and why Mr. Clinton never actually submitted the treaty to the Senate for ratification.

We've come a long distance in just a decade from the unanimous sense of the Senate regarding Kyoto to smears against skeptics that compare them to Holocaust deniers. As University of Colorado scientist Kevin Vranes, who is not a global-warming skeptic, has written:

. . . I am starting to hear . . . internal backlash [from climate scientists]. . . . None of this is to say that the risk of climate change is being questioned or downplayed by our community; it's not. It is to say that some people feel that we've created a monster by limiting the ability of people in our community to question the results that say "climate change is right here!"[35]

Skepticism is not heresy, and even if it were, how on earth do orthodox believers in global warming justify comparing heretics to Nazi sympathizers?

One skeptic who has been all but burned at the stake is Bjørn Lomborg, an adjunct professor at Denmark's Copenhagen Business School and the author of a controversial 2001 book, *The Skeptical Environmentalist*. What was controversial about the book? Simply this: that a man self-described as "Danish, liberal, vegetarian, a former member of Greenpeace" (although he later admitted that he had only contributed to Greenpeace) disagrees with the environmental "consensus." When he set out to confirm that consensus, Dr. Lomborg tells us, he found a "different picture":

We're not running out of energy or natural resources. There is ever more food, and fewer people are starving. In 1900, the average life expectancy was 30 years; today it is 67. We have reduced poverty more in the past 50 years than we did in the preceding 500. Air pollution in the industrialized world has declined—in London the air has never been cleaner since medieval times.[36]

Well, you can imagine the reaction of the environmental Inquisition. In his own country, *The Skeptical Environmentalist* was denounced by something called the Danish Committee on Scientific Dishonesty, and pressure was brought upon his English publisher, Cambridge University Press, to suppress the book.[37] The Committee on Scientific Dishonesty attacked Lomborg and the United States in its report, which asserts that the only good reviews of the book came from "leading American newspapers and [the British magazine] *The Economist*. The USA is the society with the highest energy consumption in the world, and there are powerful interests in the USA bound up with increasing energy consumption and with the belief in market forces."[38]

What that has to do with the arguments in Dr. Lomborg's work is not entirely clear.* In any case, it is true that many publications condemned the book. One that did not—the free-market review of science, *The New Atlantis*—sums up the negative reaction as "very often engaged in truly stunning, and purely ideologically-motivated, distortion."[39] *Science*, *Nature*, and *Scientific American*—arguably the most prestigious scientific publications in America—attacked the book "with sharp critiques that later turned out to be factually flawed."[40] *Scientific American* in particular went after Lomborg with remarkable vehemence, employing an editorial and four reviews, all by activists. Two of those activists were actually directly criticized in *The Skeptical Environmentalist*, and including them in the review process was highly irregular. *Scientific American* refused to include any peer review essays in support of Lomborg and would not acknowledge his

---

*The Committee's report, *The Economist* itself concluded, "objectively speaking—is incompetent and shameful."

own lengthy, point-by-point response to the magazine's criticism of him—except by threatening to sue him for copyright violation (because he quoted extensively from the *Scientific American* articles in his online response).

An editorial in *The New Atlantis* concludes:

> In itself, this story of smear campaigns and rank dishonesty by prominent scientists in the service of ideological dogma has much to teach us about the limits of scientific objectivity and the passions bubbling just beneath the surface of many scientific controversies. But more importantly, the Lomborg affair should serve as a cautionary note to an environmental movement that has long since parted ways with the facts of global ecology, and wedded itself instead to a distinctly left-ist ideology that rejects the prosperous and industrious Western way of life more than it concerns itself with the state of the environment.[41]

And, as it happens, the Danish Ministry of Science overturned the Committee on Scientific Dishonesty's report, calling it "completely void of argumentation."[42]

Bjørn Lomborg is hardly the only free-marketeer to be on the receiving end of liberal smears. Frederick Seitz was for seven years the president of the prestigious National Academy of Sciences, but when he signed a petition letter (circulated by the Oregon Institute of Science and Medicine's Petition Project) recommending the rejection of the Kyoto Protocol, the editors of *Environmental Health Perspectives* wrote that "Seitz's petition reminds us of the approach used by the tobacco industry over the decades when asked if tobacco is addictive and harmful."[43]

Understand, Dr. Seitz is a respected physicist, president for ten years of Rockefeller University, and the recipient of more than thirty honorary degrees. The comment about tobacco is especially interesting, since as president of Rockefeller Dr. Seitz did accept research funds from the R.J. Reynolds Company, one of the largest cigarette producers. This was the basis for a *Vanity Fair* article headlined:

SCIENTIST WHO SPEARHEADED ATTACKS ON GLOBAL WARMING ALSO DIRECTED $45M TOBACCO INDUSTRY EFFORT TO HIDE THE HEALTH IMPACTS OF SMOKING[44]

As Nick Schulz points out at TechCentralStation.com, this is unlikely.[45] Schulz actually spoke to the ninety-four-year-old Seitz, who said of *Vanity Fair*'s claims: "That's ridiculous, completely wrong. The money was all spent on basic science, medical research." And when Schulz asked Dr. Seitz if he ever spent money debunking the link between smoking and health, the answer was an emphatic no.

This didn't stop California's Attorney General, Bill Lockyer, from adding Dr. Seitz's name to a list of climate skeptics included in a subpoena issued to automakers. These skeptics, the subpoena says, play a "major role in spreading disinformation about global warming." (Another way of looking at statements of skepticism, of course, might be as the natural expression of free inquiry.) California's action was in response to a suit brought by automakers challenging the state's emissions standards for certain vehicles.

In a pre-trial discovery motion, California and the environmental groups asked for:

All DOCUMENTS relating to both GLOBAL WARM-ING and to any of the following individuals: S. Fred Singer, James Glassman, David Legates, Richard Lindzen, Patrick J. Michaels, Thomas Gale Moore, Robert C. Balling, Jr., Sherwood B. Idso, Craig D. Idso, Keith E. Idso, Sallie Baliunas, Paul Reiter, Chris Homer, Ross McKitrick, Julian Morris, Frederick Seitz, Willie Soon, and Steven Milloy, including but not limited to:

a. All DOCUMENTS relating to any communications between YOU and these individuals, and

b. All DOCUMENTS relating to YOUR relationship (or the relationship of any automobile manufacturer or association of automobile manufacturers) with any of them, including but not limited to payments directly or indirectly from YOU or any other automobile manufacturer or association of automobile manufacturers to any of them.[46]

Liberals often speak about the "chilling" effects of the suppression of free speech, but this is exactly what the state's subpoena does by associating the listed individuals with "disinformation." To accuse scientists of that is a smear. As the attorneys for the automakers properly pled to the court:

The so-called "climate skeptics" are not on trial in this case, and the court should resist defendants' attempt to put them on trial. Nor does this case require the court definitively to resolve questions regarding "GLOBAL WARMING" writ large. At most, as Plaintiffs have stated before and will state again at the risk of redundancy, the only relevant issue in this case with respect to global warming is the much narrower issue of what impact, if any, the [proposed emissions standards] . . . will have on global warming. . . . In the context of this battle-of-experts, Defendants' attempt to plumb the plaintiffs' files for documents regarding Defendants' hit-list of "climate skeptics" is beside the point.[47]

Indeed, some 17,000 scientists have associated themselves with the Petition Project's report on the Kyoto Protocol, a peer-reviewed paper titled, "Environmental Effects of Increased Atmospheric Carbon Dioxide." To a more temperate observer this might indicate that the "consensus" is not so broad as its advocates suggest.[48] It's worth recalling Michael Crichton's observation quoted in Chapter 1: "There is no such thing as consensus science. If it's consensus, it isn't science. If it's science, it isn't consensus. Period."

Still, even usually sober scientists can get a little pixilated when the media keep pouring out the consensus story. In a three-month survey of global-warming stories conducted by the Media Research Center, only two of fifty-one suggested that there was anything but consensus on the subject.[49] As Thomas Sowell puts it: "The left's favorite argument is that there is no argument." He suggests that if one heard both sides, "you might not be so willing to go along with those who are prepared to ruin the economy, sacrificing jobs and the national standard of living on the altar of the latest unending series of crusades, conducted by politicians and other people seeking to tell everyone else how to live."[50]

As Prof. Sowell points out, a recent book by Dennis Avery and Fred Singer pretty much says it all in its title: *Unstoppable Global*

Warming: Every 1,500 Years (2007), which explains that the earth is warming by virtue of a recurring natural cycle, that the effects of this warming trend will not be particularly dangerous, and that, anyway, since it's occurring naturally, we couldn't stop it if we wanted to.

Biting the Hand That Feeds

We've seen how attacks on fast-food restaurants have been glorified in liberal media, but McDonald's is hardly alone in being the target of elaborate and ongoing smears. Consider Wal-Mart.

The *Wall Street Journal* recently dubbed the world's leading "big-box" retailer the "Democratic Party's favorite piñata."[51] In the peculiar logic of the left, Wal-Mart is successful because it exploits the poor by offering them low prices. In a *Nation* magazine article, Liza Featherstone quotes Al Zack, a recently retired vice president of the United Food and Commercial Workers:

> [Zack] observes that appealing to the poor was "Sam Walton's real genius. He figured out how to make money off of poverty. He located his first stores in poor rural areas and discovered a real market. The only problem with the business model is that it really needs to create more poverty to grow." That problem is cleverly solved by creating more bad jobs worldwide. . . . Wal-Mart's stingy compensation policies . . . contribute to an economy in which, increasingly, workers can only afford to shop at Wal-Mart.[52]

Featherstone claims that Wal-Mart workers make, on average, $8 per hour. In fact, the current national average (Featherstone's piece ran in 2005) for full-time Wal-Mart employees is $10.11. The current federal minimum hourly wage is $5.85,[53] but Featherstone would not want us to focus on that. Instead, she writes: "Wal-Mart must keep labor costs down. It does this by making corporate crime an integral part of its business strategy."

She offers no evidence of actual criminal activity but does list a range of civil lawsuits brought by labor that challenge the retailer's overtime and other operational policies. No doubt some of the complaints have merit, but none constitutes a crime or else Wal-Mart executives would be under indictment, which they are not. She also charges Wal-Mart with being anti-woman, but some recent awards presented to the company would seem to dispute the charge:

> In 2006, Wal-Mart received the following accolades: *Black Enterprise Magazine*'s Top 30 Companies for Diversity; *DiversityInc*'s Top 10 Companies for African Americans; *DiversityInc*'s Noteworthy Companies for Diversity; *Asian Enterprise Magazine*'s Top Companies for Asian Americans; National Association of Women Lawyers' President's Award for Diversity Initiatives; *Black MBAs Magazine*'s Top 50 Companies for African American MBAs; *Hispanic Magazine*'s 2006 Corporate 100 Best Places to Work for Latinos; *LATINA Style Magazine*'s 50 Best Companies for Latinas.[54]

Despite all this, the WakeUpWalMart.com Web site continually harps on the retailer's alleged misbehavior. Referring to contributions to politicians and PACS, the Web site says:

> For a long time, we have known Wal-Mart's policies are morally corrupt, but now we are discovering Wal-Mart's politics are corrupting our government too. Have we really

hit the point in our nation's history when the world's largest corporation, Wal-Mart, and the President are willing to sell out America's children over money?[55]

The point at issue was that teenaged employees were sometimes allowed to operate chain saws, forklifts, and scrap-paper balers, which are on the Department of Labor's list of hazardous equipment not to be used by minors. In fact, Wal-Mart was fined more than $135,000 for allowing this, and it signed a compliance agreement requiring all store managers to abide by the federal law in the future.[56]

WakeUpWalMart has also gone so far as to call Wal-Mart CEO Lee Scott "corrupt" and "morally debased," as it did recently in TV ads. But WakeUpWalMart and another anti-Wal-Mart group called Wal-Mart Watch are both run by unions angry at Wal-Mart for not unionizing its 1.3 million workers: WakeUp was founded by the United Food and Commercial Workers Union, and Wal-Mart Watch is run by the Service Employees International Union.[57] "Alas," writes the *Wall Street Journal*, "what's good for working families isn't always good news for unions and their bosses." Specifically—and *pace* Featherstone—that hourly average wage paid by Wal-Mart is actually "more than many of its unionized competitors offer."

Meanwhile, let's consider what the *Wall Street Journal* describes as the real Wal-Mart Effect, which has been to

increase the purchasing power of working families by lowering prices for groceries, prescription drugs, electronic equipment and many other products that have become modern household necessities. One study, by the economic consulting firm Global Insight, calculates that Wal-Mart saves

American households an average of $2,300 a year through
lower prices, or a $263 billion reduction in the cost of living.
That compares with $33 billion savings for low-income
families from the federal food stamp program.[58]

It's an interesting datum that two thirds of Wal-Mart's managers
began as hourly employees. The American dream lives. Except, of
course, in Hollywood.

Wal-Mart is vilified in the recent film *Wal-Mart: The High Cost
of Low Price, Outfoxed and Uncovered*, made by self-described political activist Robert Greenwald. The film's Web site describes it
as "a feature length documentary that uncovers a retail giant's assault on families and American values."[59] The idea here is that
Wal-Mart's buying power and its convenience victimizes smaller
business and thus disrupts stable communities. This is a half-
truth. Wal-Mart and other large retailers do change the local
economy when they move into an area, but the aggregate effect is
more jobs, not fewer, and much lower prices, which benefits the
entire community but especially the poor.

Meanwhile, the specific example Greenwald used at the start
of his documentary proved to be unfortunate. A hardware store
owner relates the threat to his forty-year-old business from the
Wal-Mart being built in his Ohio town. He speaks of Middlefield as another in a list of communities "crucified" by Wal-Mart,
and Greenwald cuts to a sign indicating that H&H Hardware is
indeed liquidating. There is talk of monopoly and the need for
government action to stop the spread of the huge, all-consuming
retailer. But there's just one problem: H&H went out of business
three months before Wal-Mart came to Middlefield, and in an
interview with *National Review* the owner of H&H, Don Hunter,

says: "Really, there was no connection," between Wal-Mart and the demise of H&H. "I've seen a lot of small local entities wiped out because of Wal-Mart. It happens all over, but that was not the case here."[60] And that's the pattern in Greenwald's film: small distortions of facts and selective presentation of data are massaged into a horror story, as Byron York has written:

> In the end, many of the arguments against Wal-Mart presented in *The High Cost of Low Price* fail for one unavoidable reason: Wal-Mart appears at or near the top of nearly every index of corporate activity in the United States, including the bad ones, not because it is a particularly evil corporation, as Greenwald would have viewers believe, but because it is ranked near the top of everything. A lot of low-income workers? Yes—out of a workforce of 1.3 million. A big effect on local economies? Yes—just like when any other $285 billion company comes to town. A lot of crime in parking lots? Yes—out of 100 million customer visits per week. Wal-Mart's problems are not unlike those of other big-box retailers; they're just bigger.[61]

Much as scholars from the American Enterprise Institute were accused of bribing scientists to write anti-global-warming essays, so too have think-tank researchers been smeared with the charge of accepting funds from Wal-Mart in return for writing favorable articles about the retailer. Here is the lead of a feature article in the *New York Times*:

> As Wal-Mart Stores struggles to rebut criticism from unions and Democratic leaders, the company has discovered a reli-

able ally: prominent conservative research groups like the American Enterprise Institute, the Heritage Foundation and the Manhattan Institute.

Top policy analysts at these groups have written newspaper opinion pieces around the country supporting Wal-Mart, defended the company in interviews with reporters and testified on its behalf before government committees in Washington.

But the groups—and their employees—have consistently failed to disclose a tie to the giant discount retailer: financing from the Walton Family Foundation, which is run by the Wal-Mart founder Sam Walton's three children, who have a controlling stake in the company.[62]

John McWhorter of the Manhattan Institute replied indignantly, and justifiably so, in an article in the *New York Sun* titled "I Love My Think-Tank." He wrote:

Last Friday I opened the *Times* to be greeted by a photo of me illustrating a story arguing that conservative think tanks instruct their writers to shill for corporations that give them contributions. My sin was saying on a radio show a year ago (in passing amidst a discussion of several issues) that Wal-Mart provides jobs for lower-income black people. At least the photo was good—black don't crack! However, the notion that the Manhattan Institute sits its writers down and instructs us to speak in favor of corporations that give us money is fiction.

I had no idea Wal-Mart was one of our funders and have never been apprised of a list of such—nor have any of my colleagues. Rather, naturally as someone employed by a free-market think tank, I do not see Wal-Mart as the scourge to humanity that it has become fashionable to claim. The less-than-generous health insurance they offer is a problem, and to me suggests a new discussion about national health insurance. But I said Wal-Mart offers gainful employment to poor blacks because it is, quite simply, true, as plenty of black community representatives have been noting for years.[63]

The smear was doubly disheartening to McWhorter, because the implications were that the conservative Manhattan Institute was dishonest and that he, as a black man, was a tool of (his phrase) "white plutocrats." People are entitled to their differing opinions, he wrote: "But when I express mine, it won't be because my "patron" told me to, and I will say to them loudly: I'm black, I work for the Manhattan Institute, and I'm proud."

For its part, the *Times* issued a correction:

The *Times* article said that the groups and their employees had consistently failed to disclose the donations, and it said in the first paragraph that the Manhattan Institute for Policy Research was one of them. But a Manhattan Institute author had told *The Times* that he had indeed disclosed contributions from the Walton Foundation in an article he wrote, a fact that should have been included in the *Times* article.

The article also reported that Tim Kane of the Heritage Foundation and Karl Zinsmeister, formerly of the American Enterprise Institute, were among those who wrote articles favorable to Wal-Mart after their foundations received a donation.

Both those groups were called for comment for the *Times* article. Mr. Kane, who was not called, subsequently said that he did not know about the Walton Family Foundation contribution and that he had criticized Wal-Mart's call for a higher federal minimum wage in an article he wrote. The *Times* also did not ask Mr. Zinsmeister to comment, but he declined to do so when reached after the *Times* article was published. Both Mr. Kane and Mr. Zinsmeister should have been asked to comment before publication.[64]

The correction, which I have quoted at length—although not in its entirety—may seem innocuous, but in fact it is a damning commentary by the paper on its own journalistic practices, and it makes clear the agenda of the reporters with regard to Wal-Mart.

One other think-tank veteran, the often-quoted-here Thomas Sowell of the Hoover Institution, wrote:

I could not name five donors to [Hoover] if my life depended on it, though I am sure there are far more than five. For all I know, I may have defended some of those unknown donors—or I may have bitten the hand that feeds me by attacking them. . . .

Such cheap-shot journalism tells us more about those who engage in it, and the constituency to which they appeal, than about those they write about. It tells us there are people so narrow and shallow they cannot understand how anyone else could possibly disagree with what they believe without having sold out.[65]

But, like Mr. McWhorter, Prof. Sowell has never sold out to anybody.

Some final words on Wal-Mart. If it were a country, it would have the twentieth largest economy on the planet. When a new store was going to open recently in Glendale, Arizona, Wal-Mart received eight thousand applications for the store's five hundred-plus jobs, and this is typical of the response the company receives when it moves into a new town. And, as Kevin Hassett reports for Bloomberg News, the benefits generally overcome the attacks against the company:

> There's no question that the thuggish attempt to smear and intimidate imposes harsh costs on Wal-Mart. But the money trail reminds us, more than anything, why unionization has had so much trouble taking hold in the U.S.
>
> Imagine if you worked at Wal-Mart and saw your employer demonized by these people. Would it make you want to join the union? The high-tech goons the unions have sicced on Wal-Mart are employing exactly the types of tactics that have given unions a bad name.[66]

Of course liberal advocacy groups such as MoveOn.org and the aforementioned WakeUpWalMart and Wal-Mart Watch Internet sites have strongly endorsed Greenwald's film, and, like the unions that support them, they dislike the power of large companies such as Wal-Mart. But as Professor Sowell has written:

> [J]ust what does the vague word "power" mean when it comes to business? Wal-Mart is the big bugaboo these days but what "power" does Wal-Mart have? I lived three-quarters of a century without ever setting foot in a Wal-Mart store and there is not a thing they can do about it.[67]

Except, he might have added, *whine.*

Although it's a better topic for this book's next chapter, it seems right to point out here that the often-smeared "dead-end" jobs at Wal-Mart or McDonald's or any other enterprise aren't that at all. For young people, people without much education, and for retired people these jobs are lifesavers.

Lego My Legos

We end this chapter with a consideration of one of the more remarkable smears against enterprise, entrepreneurship, and capitalism in recent memory: the banning of Legotown by the Hilltop Children's Center in Seattle.

Many of us, especially if we are parents, are familiar with Legos, the colorful interlocking blocks used by kids to construct anything and everything from castles to spaceships. But at Hilltop, an after-school child-care program, some teachers were dismayed by the effect the creativity toys had on their five- through nine-year-olds. They became competitive while playing, and their Legotown—an ongoing project by the kids—began to lead some of the children to behave selfishly and even rudely toward others. Some claimed ownership of the Legos and the structures they had built. As any parent or teacher knows, this is what kids do. But at Hilltop, the teachers started noticing that

> Into their coffee shops and houses, the children were building their assumptions about ownership and the social power it conveys—assumptions that mirrored those of a class-based, capitalist society—a society that we teachers believe to be unjust and oppressive. As we watched the children build, we became increasingly concerned.[68]

The teachers held a sort of sixties-style encounter group in which they discussed this. And then one weekend some children at the church building where Hilltop is located accidentally damaged the Legotown. This gave the teachers an opportunity— a "teachable moment," as some on the Left like to call it—to "launch a critical evaluation of . . . the inequities of private ownership and hierarchical authority upon which it was founded. Our intention was to promote a contrasting set of values: collectivity, collaboration, resource-sharing, and full democratic participation."

Let's not even pause to consider the difference between teaching and *promoting*.

The teachers proudly noted how uncomfortable this made the kids who had been leaders in Legotown:

> These children seemed to squirm at the implications of privilege, wealth, and power that "giving" holds. The children denied their power, framing it as benign and neutral, not something actively sought out and maintained.

As a father I can only say I wouldn't have wanted to be the parent of the glassy-eyed eight-year-old who came home from school after one of the boys allowed as how he actually liked having power, because it made him feel free. The teachers were startled, they have written, by the "raw truth" of the little boy's confession, and that really set them to work:

> Drew's comment startled us with its raw truth. He was a member of the Legotown inner circle, and had been quite resistant to acknowledging the power he held in that role.

Using Drew's "breakthrough," they changed the rules of the game, so that some of the former leaders now had less valuable Legos, and former outsiders had the most prized pieces.

> Drew said, "I stopped trading because the same people were winning. I just gave up." In the game, the children could experience what they'd not been able to acknowledge in Legotown: When people are shut out of participation in the power structure, they are disenfranchised—and angry, discouraged, and hurt.

As one blogger summarized the Hilltop teachers' smear of capitalism: "Basically, they are instilling in the children that capitalism, a system in which people own their own land and property, is bad and oppressive. . . . This time it's just at an unbelievably early age."[69]

So much for preparing kids for the real world, let alone for educating them about the virtues of enterprise and the necessity of leadership.

VI

SHINING THROUGH
A Depreciation of Smear Tactics

Listen to what the red state citizens say about themselves, the songs they write, and the sermons they flock to. They know who they are—they are full of original sin and they have a taste for violence. The blue state citizens make the Rousseauvian mistake of thinking humans are essentially good, and so they never realize when they are about to be slugged from behind.

—Novelist Jane Smiley, commenting
on the results of the 2004 election[1]

I HAD ORIGINALLY INTENDED TO CALL this last chapter "Smear Tactics: An Obituary." Then I researched and mostly wrote the book, and realized that there is simply no way Americans on opposing sides of various contentious issues will ever bury the hatchet—except maybe in each other's backs. Political and social tensions anger people, and angry people—especially if they are ideological—will resort to smear tactics.

So does this mean I despair? Not really. I accept the laws of reality. Therefore, instead of an obituary, this will be a *depreciation*.*

Among those laws I respect: In a democracy various interest

---

*As opposed to an *appreciation*.

groups will compete for power. They always have. From the very beginning the Founders worried about it—about what they called *factions*. They knew there would be factions, shifting majorities and minorities jockeying for power, and that the competition among them could and probably would be cutthroat. This part is nothing new.

James Madison wrote about this in Federalist No. 10, generally considered the most significant of the Federalist Papers that he, John Jay, and Alexander Hamilton wrote during the summer and fall of 1787 to convince Americans of the soundness of the new nation conceived of in the Constitution—and to win ratification for the Constitution. He and Hamilton especially were visionaries: they knew their young, small nation would mature into a very great state, and they needed to overcome the belief, widely held at the time, that republican* government simply wasn't possible in a large nation. Large nations, so the thinking went, would be torn apart by factionalism. The Anti-Federalists admired the theories of the French writer Montesquieu (author of the influential *The Spirit of the Laws*), who believed that a republic had to be geographically small and culturally unified to survive. In No. 9, however, Hamilton refuted the Anti-Federalists (who opposed the proposed Constitution) by pointing out that the great Frenchman considered even the American states too large, and by reminding his readers that the new American government would be simply a federation of those states, after all, and not a super-state. The powers of the national government were to be both well-defined and, more important, limited.

---

*We live in a republic, not a democracy. Leaders are elected democratically by—it is to be hoped—virtuous citizens: free people who live by the rule of law. The individual right of citizens do not derive from government but are protected by government.

Madison picked up Hamilton's argument in No. 10, reasoning that the republic as outlined was the best guarantor of individual liberties (and minority interests) against the power of those shifting majorities. The checks and balances in the Constitution would protect against "the mischief of faction." In Madison's view, Americans should not expect to be of one mind about the issues of the day, and should even expect to be put off by the "vicious arts" of endless politicking. But—and it's a big *but*—the very size and diversity of the American population under republican aegis would tend to prevent the kind of factionalism that he and Hamilton assumed were the natural consequence of pure democracy. They knew—but didn't say—that in a democracy in which every idea and institution was constantly in play and in which decisions would be made ad hoc, nothing of true value would be left in place over time; that you very well might have somebody credibly call for a show of hands about the Ten Commandments. Should we only have eight? How about running the number to fifteen? Let's vote!

That was then. But even then, the Anti-Federalists raised some powerful and enduring questions about the future nation they could seen glinting in the eyes of the Federalists. They feared that the national government was destined to grow to unmanageable size and that the states would end up in one or another sort of clash. The Anti-Federalist called "Cato" (the Federalists used the name "Publius" in their essays) wrote that "the difference of extent, and number of inhabitants . . . the dissimilitude of interest, morals, and policies . . . will in its exercise, emphatically be, like a house divided against itself."

This was seventy-three years *before* the outbreak of the Civil War.

Did that war and subsequent history settle the matter? Well, with regard to slavery and some other issues, yes, but we're still at each other's throats. And it seems to me that one missing element in our understanding of the checks-and-balances character of the American system is what the founding generation and most subsequent generations assumed was behind both the Federalist and Anti-Federalist arguments: that once upon a time we agreed more than we disagreed, because we agreed about life's premises. And what's different now—and what's causing the deteriorating climate of the American conversation about politics, religion, and so many topics large and small—is that the liberals (the ones truly on the historical Left) are not on the same page as the rest of us, and the truth is they never have been—not even when they first emerged in earnest within a generation after the American Founding. And what's more ominous is this: never before have they been as influential as they are today.

We recently lived through the so-called Reagan Revolution, which to many people seemed to have begun a kind of purification of American politics, in the sense of a return of the nation to policies more closely in tune with the principles of the American Founding. To some extent Ronald Reagan and his followers probably did begin such a process, but it is far from certain that it will continue or that the greatest number of Americans want it to continue. Probably, however, they do.

Opinion polls are not necessarily sound measures of cultural and political reality, but it is certainly compelling that consistently over the last several decades the researchers have found that when Americans are asked to self-identify politically, between 15 and 20 percent describe themselves as liberal, about 35 percent say they are moderate, and as many as 41 percent call themselves conservative.[2] That being the case, why on earth don't Republicans triumph in every single election? Well, for starters, the political-party breakdown is more balanced: about one third each are Republican, Democrat, or Independent. Political outcomes are determined by those more moderate Independents, who may seem to sway in the sociopolitical winds. They elected Reagan; they elected Bill Clinton. They put the GOP in charge in 1994 and threw them out in 2006. This political ebb and flow is not likely to change when big issues—the Iraq war, for instance—are associated with one or another party.* Still, it seems fair to say that the Republicans tend to be the party of the status quo and the Democrats the party of change—the one is conservative and the other (to use the word liberals have come to prefer) *progressive*. One is the party of Normalcy and the other of the New Deal. Everybody knows this is rank simplification, but it is true in some sense—in the sense of what folks used to call the Big Picture, which is pretty much the way we perceive things in the Age of Media.

It has been this way since the 1930s, although between about 1948 and 1968 the real, functional differences between Republicrats and Democrans were as hard to distinguish as Rosencrantz from Gildenstern. And this was partly the legacy of another innovation of the Founding Generation: the Electoral College.

Because we have a system requiring that the winner of every presidential election must receive a majority of the votes of the Electoral College, a two-party political system has evolved to guarantee that outcome. Results such as those in the early years of

*Speaking of polls, they show that even on the eve of the great 1994 Republican Restoration party affiliation favored Democrats. The big difference in 2006 was the movement of Independents away from the GOP.

the Republic, which threw decision making into the House of Representatives, were too traumatic and divisive, and at least since the Civil War third-party candidates have done little more than highlight the inevitability of Republican and Democratic power sharing—and not only in the serial handoff of the presidency, but in congressional seats as well.* Some commentators have lately suggested that the White House has largely become the province of the GOP, and yet since 1960 the split is essentially equal: In a dozen elections, the GOP has an edge of a single victory, which in 2000 was arguably the narrowest possible, with George W. Bush winning *only* in the Electoral College. It has also become fashionable to denounce the Electoral College because of that outcome, but this is shortsighted.

It has been the genius of America's constitutional system that the Electoral College has not only all but mandated two parties but has forced them to be—so some say—Tweedledum and Tweedledee. Or Tweedle Dumb and Dumber. This is an understandable and, at times, laudable sort of cynicism, until you realize that it's the two-party system that has kept Americans united politically for so long.

But that sense of unity may be collapsing today; it's certainly under pressure, and most of the discontent about the two-party system comes from the Left.

The fact that self-identified liberals represent the smallest group in the liberal-moderate-conservative breakdown in opinion polls would seem to suggest that splintering off into a third, lib-

---

*It may well be that in 1992 billionaire Ross Perot's candidacy under the banner of the Reform Party cost George H. W. Bush reelection as President. At one point during the campaign, Perot even led in the polls, although he ended up with just 18.9 percent of the popular vote and no electoral votes.

eral political party would serve only to guarantee that thunder would be stolen from whomever the Democrats nominate for president, with the likely outcome of a GOP victory. In New York, there is a tradition of smaller parties making a challenge to the major parties, and in 1970 the political world was shocked by the election to the U.S. Senate of James L. Buckley, older brother of William F. Buckley Jr., who was the Conservative Party candidate. (Jim Buckley beat Republican incumbent Charles Godell and Democratic challenger Richard Ottinger. He lost his reelection bid in 1976 to a centrist Democrat, Daniel Patrick Moynihan.) But Buckley's election was arguably the highlight of the history of New York's Conservative Party, which today has lost much of its effectiveness and, like its Liberal Party counterpart, struggles to maintain its position on the state's ballot. Indeed, since the 2002 election, the Liberal Party has all but ceased to exist, and the Conservative Party's fortunes have declined substantially—largely because it is perceived to have become little more than a rubber stamp of the GOP's gubernatorial nominees. Eleven different parties were represented in New York's 2006 statewide elections, with six different candidates in the gubernatorial race, won overwhelmingly by the Democrats' Eliot Spitzer. Only the Green Party candidate, author Malachy McCourt, received as much as 1 percent of the vote, and the splinter candidacies had no effect on the election's result. Ninety-eight percent of all votes cast in the governor's race were for the candidates of the two national parties.* Candidates from the Green, Socialist, Libertarian, and Independent (as opposed to Independence) parties

---

*GOP candidate John Faso also received the Conservative Party nomination, just as Spitzer received the nod from both the Independence and Working Families parties.

had their day in the sun, of course, and were able to influence some voters, but—as in national races—it was good old Tweedledum and Tweedledee in the end.

A Meaningful Digression About Who We Are

It's always tempting to pose the question: Who are we really? We are Americans. And during the period from the election of Ronald Reagan until the election of 2006, when the GOP's fortunes took a downward turn, it seemed possible to answer that Americans are mostly conservative; that America itself is a conservative nation. I did so in the introduction I wrote to an earlier book called *Good Order*, which was published in 1995. My endorsement of the idea was pretty tentative—or possibly indecisive—and this was largely because defining conservatism (or liberalism) is a fool's task. Nobody really agrees on any precise meaning for most political terms, and I wrote then that it would be lovely to have a test of political stance—a Worldview Quotient much like the Intelligence Quotient with which we're all familiar:

> Some conservatives might speculate that a WQ distribution curve would look like a wave swelling from left to right and breaking after passing center. But, if so, how far after? . . . [T]he truth is probably not as far right as many liberals fear, more centered than most conservatives hope.[3]

The fact is that Americans as a whole, as a people, do cluster around the "center"—however ill-defined that center may be. When the pollsters ask us to self-identify according to one of the three descriptors—liberal, moderate, or conservative—they are making a fundamental, if inevitable error. What error? Consider this: Whereas one can at least begin to define liberalism and conservatism, and can identify liberal and conservative philosophers, politicians, and personalities, it's far more difficult to name a philosopher of moderatism or list the principles thereof. The labeling is a bit easier in a purely electoral context, wherein candidates appeal for the votes of registered Democrats, Republicans, and Independents, or even in pre-election polls wherein surveys gauge the leanings of those favoring or opposing a candidate or an issue with those who are "undecided."

And, speaking historically, those whom we call *conservatives* in America today are actually *liberals*, although they are better thought of as "classical liberals." In fact, I'd be in favor of abandoning the term *conservative* in favor of *classical liberal*, were it not for the fact that "conservative" has—thanks to an estimable cadre of writers and activists, especially from the middle of the 20th century on—become by customary usage the preferred word. And as the blurred distinction between "conservative" and "liberal" suggests, we hardly need to go looking for new words that very well may do nothing but put us into a denser fog of meaning and understanding.

Enlightenment

Probably no era in human history—and certainly in the history of the West—has been more influential than the period we now call the Enlightenment, which is to say the 18th century. It has been called the Age of Reason (or in France *Le Siècle de Lumières*).[4] In fact, the revolution in ideas the Enlightenment represents has its roots in antiquity and in existential awareness and no doubt in

events of the preceding period, most notably in the English Revolution of 1688, and we know it today because we know ourselves.
It culminated in two great events, which represent the paths Enlightenment took as it moved forward in time: the American and
French revolutions. The first "revolution" was a movement for republican democracy; the second, for all the ideals it may have
seemed to share with its American counterpart, was a descent into
totalitarian terror. Both began in violence, but in America the violence ended with the establishment of the new nation.

In France, however, the violence escalated into class war.*

In America, Americans modified their English traditions to
create a new nation, "conceived in Liberty," as Abraham Lincoln
would say four score and seven years after the fact, "and dedicated
to the proposition that all men are created equal."

In France, the Jacobins sought a kind of tabula rasa in which
every basic institution of French life was swept away by a theory.
It was an age of reason, perhaps, but one in which reason had
become untethered: "Reason in this context meant human speculation unguided by experience or prescription; the a priori assumption toppling the a posteriori tradition; agnosticism defrocking
faith."[5]

---

*In *Do As I Say (Not As I DO)* (Doubleday, 2005), Peter Schweizer writes about the
"world's greatest intellectual," MIT linguistics professor Noam Chomsky, one of
whose books was famously brandished during a UN speech by Venezuelan dictator
Hugo Chavez. One of the most persistent themes in Chomsky's work has been class
warfare. He has frequently lashed out against the "massive use of tax havens to shift
the burden to the general population and away from the rich" and criticized the
concentration of wealth in "trusts" by the wealthiest 1 percent. The American tax
code is rigged with "complicated devices for ensuring that the poor—like 80 percent of the population—pay off the rich." But trusts can't be all bad. After all, as
Schweizer reports, Chomsky, with a net worth north of $2,000,000, decided to cre-
ate one for himself.

As novelist Charles Dickens wrote about the period of the Jacobins* in *A Tale of Two Cities*—and he might have been describing our own time:

It was the best of times, it was the worst of times, it was the age of wisdom, it was the age of foolishness, it was the epoch of belief, it was the epoch of incredulity, it was the season of Light, it was the season of Darkness, it was the spring of hope, it was the winter of despair, we had everything before us, we had nothing before us, we were all going direct to Heaven, we were all going direct the other way—in short, *the period was so far like the present period, that some of its noisiest authorities insisted on its being received, for good or for evil, in the superlative degree of comparison only.* [Emphasis added.]

There were two writers who fairly represent the directions taken by the philosophy of the Enlightenment into the future: Jean-Jacques Rousseau (1712–1778), whose thinking culminates in Karl Marx and those who follow that worldview today, and Edmund Burke (1729–1797), whose work reflects America's founding principles and who is considered the founding father of what we call conservatism, but which is really just classical liberalism—with an added dimension of Christian prudence.

*The Jacobins were members of a club of French revolutionaries, the most famous of whom was Maximilien Robespierre. The Jacobin Club was arguably the birthplace of true left-wing politics—a designation derived originally from their seating position in the Estates General. The Jacobins led the Terror that guillotined so many. Ironically, they took their name from their meeting place, the Dominican convent of St. James (*Jacobus*) in Paris.

Prudence was not Rousseau's forte. For all his undeniable genius (he was a philosopher, novelist, composer, and educator), he was a proto-totalitarian. He believed that tradition is simply another name for slavery and famously believed that the people must be "forced to be free" and that freedom was found in what he called the "general will."

> In order then that the social compact may not be an empty formula, it tacitly includes the undertaking, which alone can give force to the rest, that whoever refuses to obey the general will shall be compelled to do so by the whole body. This means nothing less than that he will be forced to be free; for this is the condition which, by giving each citizen to his country, secures him against all personal dependence. In this lies the key to the working of the political machine; this alone legitimizes civil undertakings, which, without it, would be absurd, tyrannical, and liable to the most frightful abuses.[6]

As it happened, of course, true tyranny arose from those who advocated one or another version of the "general will" (as in the dictatorship of the proletariat), and the oxymoronic notion of forcing people to be free is simply a justification for an elite to assert its enlightened view on everybody else—a way, especially, to trample underfoot any tradition deemed inimical to the progressive theory. What's more, Rousseau is often credited with being the champion of subjectivity—of believing there is no reality that isn't self-created; of being certain that Man not God determines the basic laws organizing civil society; of believing that Man is perfectible; of being the champion of an avant-garde, the elite required to lead the people by reason and science. He truly is the patron of modern academia.

Edmund Burke, on the other hand, whose most famous book was his *Reflections on the Revolution in France*, embraced the era's nascent liberalism without jettisoning traditional mores or, especially, its religious ethics. He has been called a "Christian pessimist," who objected to the French Revolution (but not to American independence), because—as he wrote to the putative Frenchman to whom the *Reflections* is addressed—"You are now to live in a new order of things under a plan of Government of which no Man can speak from experience."[7] This he considered intolerable.

Of Burke, Lord Acton (J. E. E. Dalberg) wrote that he was conservative by virtue of his notion of history; that otherwise he was a liberal, "the first of liberals, the first of conservatives."

So what was this classical liberalism to which Burke and America's Founding Fathers adhered? It consisted, in the summation of one scholar, in:

- an ethical emphasis on the individual as a rights-bearer prior to the existence of any state, community, or society;
- the support of the right of property carried to its economic conclusion, a free market system;
- the desire for a limited constitutional government to protect individuals' rights from others and from its own expansion; and
- the universal (global and ahistorical) applicability of these above convictions.[8]

It was, of course, more than this, but in these four points, we certainly hear the echoes of Jefferson's summation in the Declara-

tion, of "self-evident" truths. Although missing is Jefferson's statement of the source of those truths: "the Laws of Nature and of
Nature's God." And implicit is the sure military conflict that
would follow from the Declaration. History notes that the earlier
draft of the Declaration used "Property" in the place of "pursuit of
Happiness" in the trio with Life and Liberty, and there you have
classical liberalism codified.

The question is: How far from the tenets of classical liberalism and the American Founders are those who today call themselves "liberals," and how close are those who call themselves
"conservatives" (those who are conventionally classically liberal)?
And is the gap between these two groups widening? And is the
gap, whether widening or not, a reason for the apparent increase
in incivility?

Of course, thinking of Jefferson, we recall that smear tactics
were as intensely practiced by the Founding Generation as by
anyone today—and, to an extent, for the same reasons. The opponents of Jefferson in particular were sure he was a Jacobin at
heart (and he certainly was among the Founders one of the most
initially sympathetic to the French Revolution), but that was a
smear. For all his faith in reason, he never believed that the "best
and the brightest" should sweep away tradition in favor of some
new insight into governance. He may or may not have observed
"that government governs best which governs least," but he definitely and specifically said: "I am certainly not an advocate for
frequent and untried changes in laws and institutions."[9] And in
an 1816 letter to his friend John Taylor he spoke of his trust in
the people, "believing, as I do, that the mass of citizens is the saf-
est depository of their own rights. . . ." He went on: "[A]nd especially, [believing] that the evils flowing from the duperies of the

people, are less injurious than those from the egoism of their agents, I am friend to that composition of government which has in it the most of this ingredient."[10]

The essence of "liberal" phenomenology—the assumption behind their arguments*—is this: There are no absolutes; therefore everything is relative; and therefore the only arbiter of what is true is *power*. The essence of conservative phenomenology is that there are absolutes; that everything must be measured against those absolutes; and that therefore truth is rooted in tradition.

But the way ahead isn't necessarily a matter of competition (whether through elections or the market) *replacing* tradition. Since people's choices reflect the complex framework of their preferences, the warp of naked self-interest may be woven with the weft of faith. Contradictions often fade away when we understand them to be threads composing the tapestry that is American society.

Traditions evolve naturally, and at no point are we ever without the sources of the traditions: the first precious filaments of that great tapestry cannot be pulled from the fabric.

Before I'm tempted to go any further with textile analogies, let me offer an example: Christian rock. As a musical genre it is not without its vociferous critics, but artists such as Amy Grant have taken traditional Protestant hymns and gospel music into the Top 40, and groups such as Petra, Servant, Third Day, and SONIC-

*Phenomenology is defined as the study of consciousness and self-awareness as a preface to a philosophy. My use of the word here is probably not particularly precise, but what I mean is, as I wrote, the *assumption behind the arguments*—the antecedent (or antecedents) to our ideas about life and liberty. Political scientist Willmoore Kendall once wrote that Americans carry Western tradition "in their hips." This is what I mean.

FLOOd have electrified audiences with their own varieties of Christian rock. The Catholic troubadour John Michael Talbot has even recorded what he calls Monk Rock from the monastery he founded in Arkansas. And if we put aside caviling about the chasm of quality that may exist between, on the one hand, the sacred music of past ages—of Gregorian chant (c. 900) or "Amazing Grace" (c. 1748)—and, on the other, Amy Grant's "El Shaddai" (1982), we can easily recognize the same spirit of love, peace, and humility in all of it.

In "God's Grandeur," the great Jesuit poet, Gerard Manley Hopkins (1844–1889), laments that generations that "have trod, have trod, have trod" upon this earth and tarnished simply *everything*. And yet:

> . . . *for all this nature is never spent;*
> *There lives the dearest freshness deep down things;*
> *And though the last lights of the black West went*
> *Oh, morning, at the brown brink, eastward, springs—*
> *Because the Holy Spirit over the bent*
> *World broods with warm breast and with ah!*
>   *bright wings.*

The soul of creation is liberty. God made us free, because love must be freely given. Although we should view ourselves and society with wariness, there are two levels of faith required for the good life—neither of them favored among elite opinion: We must have faith in God, and we must have faith in one another. We must believe in Providence and in the People.

Some conservative Christians may decry religious rock music as an inappropriate marriage of the sacred and the profane, and they are certainly entitled to their opinion in a free society. (Some may also object as a matter of aesthetic taste, but that's a different matter.) What cannot be forgotten are the sage words of Burke: "A nation without some means of change is without the means of its preservation." There never was and never will be a generation that doesn't judge the next as unworthy of the legacy of at least the one once removed, let alone the generation of the Founders.

There are many ways to view the founding of America and the men who laid the cornerstone in the great structure we are still building. They were Christians; no, they were deists. They were conservatives; no, they were liberals. They were honorable; no, they were hypocritical. And to be sure, they were complex people, and for every "on the one hand" in our debates about them and their intentions, there is an "on the other hand." And yet it seems clear that as a group they believed in Providence and the People.

Just as clearly, the contemporary Left believes in neither.

The reader will recall, I hope, that at the beginning of this book I made reference to the elites that drive the incessant bickering in American life:

> Call them elites or Mandarins or the Anointed, they are a class of postmodernist true believers who are convinced that their intelligence and their education and their philosophy have made them more capable than the rest of us to govern America. However, failing any substantial appeal to the electorate, they must maneuver for power by means of stealth.

On reflection, I'm not sure that part about stealth can be said to be true, given the amplification of elite opinion in the media. In fact, it's the very level of elite noise that has so many Americans worried about polarization.

But are we polarized? My own experience with conservatives leads me to conclude that most on the American "Right" would rather see us united than divided, and my sense of the Left is that the opposite is true for them. But what about the vast majority of Americans who are not among those elites on either end of the political continuum?

Well, according to some experts, we're pretty much one people. "Americans are closely divided," writes political scientist Morris Fiorina, "but not deeply divided. We split evenly in elections not because we are bitterly opposed camps, but because we instinctively seek the center...."[11] It's the elites, he contends, who are out on the extremes.

In the end then, what are the main differences between, on the one hand, the American Left and, on the other, some American liberals and moderates and most American conservatives?

To begin to explain this, let me indicate why I do not state the distinction as between the Left and the Right.

There really is no American Right. Not anyway in the sense in which that term is used elsewhere in the world, where it indicates either monarchical or theocratic parties.

This is not to say that some individuals don't enjoy employing the term; they do. Not for nothing does William F. Buckley Jr. call his long-running syndicated column "On the Right." But unlike the Left, which is a consciously global movement, American conservatives—however much they may be interested in foreign affairs or in universal ideas—are rooted in the particularities of the American experience. The Left believes in a kind of philosophical globalism (I don't use that word here to refer to economic policy as such), whereas conservatives believe in localism. When in a 2004 presidential debate the Democratic candidate, John Kerry, spoke of the need for aspects of American foreign policy to be validated by a "global test," he identified himself as a man of the Left, whether or not that was his intention. It is all but inconceivable—even in the era of "big-government" conservatism—that a conservative could utter such a phrase. Conservatives may have some extreme positions with regard to some issues, but the core of conservative belief—of classical liberal belief—is Americanism.

This is not true of the Left.

And I note here the anger of *The New Republic*'s David Greenberg at the way a *New York Times* article conflated leftism and liberalism.[12] In writing about the upcoming fifth anniversary of 9/11, the *Times*'s Sheryl Gay Stolberg spoke of filmmaker Michael Moore (of *Fahrenheit 9/11* fame) as a liberal, and Greenberg objected:

> Michael Moore is a leftist, not a liberal, and it's amazing that the *Times* can hold up someone of his views as 'embodying' liberal ideas. Moore is well known to be hostile to liberalism. Sure, his film had its merits, . . . [but] does any liberal fully endorse his view of 9/11? The distinction between liberalism and leftism was once widely understood. People knew that the radical left saw liberalism, even more than conservatism, as its chief enemy. Today that distinction has slipped from common understanding.[13]

Through its fantasies of oppression, its advocacy of multiculturalism, its embrace of foreign precedents in domestic legal disputes, and its endorsement of international consensus in foreign affairs, the Left demonstrates its *functional* anti-Americanism. I emphasize "functional," because the effect is almost certainly the same even if the intent is not consciously, actively unpatriotic.

And why is this so? I can only speculate. But behind it all I see the Left's passionate attachment to equality. Equality—at least as defined by the Left's policies and philosophies—diminishes differences, where, that is, it does not actually obliterate them, as was the case in the failed Soviet experiment, notwithstanding the commissars who drove imported cars and spent weekends at luxurious dachas. But make no mistake, whether in multiculturalism or in communism, the individual is either diminished or destroyed, and the individual is the basis of society.

It is a paradox of multiculturalism that it seems superficially to celebrate diversity, yet in its applications ends up erasing it. This is because multiculturalism, like its parent socialism, is based not so much upon notions of equal justice (to which no right-thinking person may object) but upon envy.

Contest and Content

"American politics" is two things: it is the ongoing *contest* of people and philosophy, and it is the *content* of America's evolving tradition. Over the last half century of American history, we have become more attentive to the former than to the latter, thanks mostly to radio and then television. Personality has trumped history.

Many now believe that what matters most is the contest; many more passively observe the contest. Too few know the content of tradition. So dominant is the contest that some believe any winning idea is ipso facto American, and victory may come in the press, in the classroom, in the courts, and—although not necessary—at the polls. To the Left, especially, power is what matters. Even "reasonable" liberals such as Ronald Dworkin of New York University, who calls for "partnership democracy," contend that majority decisions (i.e., the people's opinions) are valid only (in the summation of Peter Berkowitz) "when they meet certain philosophical tests of reasonableness and morality," which is to say when the elites say they're okay.[14]

But not every winning or powerful idea is American. Nothing is American simply by virtue of its being resident on this continent or in the mind of someone simply standing on American soil. In fact, plenty of what's printed, taught, and decided is in terms of the content of tradition un-American.

We may disagree over exactly what constitutes Americanism, about what that tradition meant historically and what it means today, but there can be no dispute that there is such a thing as Americanism, some group of notions and mores that makes America and Americans unique. This may sound self-evident, even a little silly, but it isn't. For starters, we know that Washington and Adams, Jefferson and Franklin, and the entire Founding generation set out to create a new nation, as Lincoln would say later, "conceived in Liberty, and dedicated to the proposition that all men are created equal." Forget for the moment that there was some hypocrisy among those who made the proposition; accept simply that there *was* a proposition. That in July 1776 and in November 1863 that proposition was tested in war and then in peace, and that the outcome was birth and then rebirth.

As historian David McCullough told a group of college students in 2006:

I think that we need history as much as we need bread or water or love. To make the point, I want to discuss a single human being and why we should know him. And the first thing I want to say about him is that he is an example of the transforming miracle of education. When he and others wrote in the Declaration of Independence about "life, liberty and the pursuit of happiness," what they meant by "happiness" wasn't longer vacations or more material goods. They were talking about the enlargement of the human experience through the life of the mind and the life of the spirit. And they knew that the system of government they were setting up wouldn't work if the people weren't educated. "If a nation expects to be ignorant and free, in a state of civilization," Jefferson wrote, "it expects what never was and never will be."[15]

Read the following statements and try to guess by whom and when they were written. Of course, I've left off certain clauses and words that would give away the conceit:

Our nation has entered into an age in which Divine Providence has permitted the genius of man . . .

[I]t is our prayerful hope that the people, whom we have so faithfully served, will renew the mandate to continue our service and that Almighty God may grant us the wisdom to succeed . . .

The administration of our government . . . has been based upon principles of justice and equity, and upon the American tradition of fair play. Men who are elected to high political office are entrusted with high responsibilities. Slander, defamation of character, deception and dishonesty are as truly transgressions of God's commandments, when resorted to by men in public life, as they are for all other men. . . .

Is this from: A) one of the Federalist Papers? B) one of Mr. Lincoln's speeches? or C) an early essay in *National Review*? The answer is: none of the above, although the era is pretty much the same as C. I have selectively quoted here, of course, but these stirring phrases of patriotism, faith, and morality come from the 1952 platform of . . . the Democratic Party.

The platform does contain a number of propositions that would not have made the editors of *National Review* feel easy, including its starry-eyed optimism about the United Nations as a peacekeeper, its nostalgia for the legacy of the New Deal, or its insistence upon a program of "federal rent control." On the other hand, it must have cheered conservatives to read this, under the subhead, "Support for the Victims of Soviet Imperialism":

The United States should join other nations in formally declaring genocide to be an international crime in time of peace as well as war. This crime was exposed once more by the shocking revelations of Soviet guilt as disclosed in the report filed in Congress by the special committee investigating the Katyn Forest massacre. We look forward to the day when the liberties of Poland and the other oppressed Soviet satellites, including Czechoslovakia, Hungary, Rumania, Bulgaria, Albania, Lithuania, Estonia and Latvia and other nations in Asia under Soviet domination, will be restored to them and they can again take their rightful place in the community of free nations.

And I am particularly struck by this statement concerning immigration policy, which is hardly in the spirit of the multiculturalism to come: "Subversive elements must be screened out and prevented from entering our land. . . ." And—anticipating the tax-cutting policies of John F. Kennedy that would come two presidential cycles on—the platform calls for a reduction of taxes as "rapidly as defense requirements permit," as well as "keeping government expenditures to the lowest practicable level."

It was a sign of the times that a fair portion of the document is devoted to the specifics of farm policy—in 1952, America still considered itself an agricultural nation, even as the inexorable forces of industrialization and urbanization had long since begun transforming the nation and effectively separating Americans from their agrarian past.

And now another quiz. Name the source of this quote:

> We maintain that man was not born to be ruled, but that he consented to be governed; and that the reasons that moved him thereto are few and simple. He has voluntarily submitted to government because, only by the establishment of just laws, and the power to enforce those laws, can an orderly life be maintained, full and equal opportunity for all be established, and the blessings of liberty be perpetuated.
>
> We hold that government, and those entrusted with government, should set a high example of honesty, of justice, and unselfish devotion to the public good; that they should labor to maintain tranquility at home and peace and friendship with all the nations of the earth.

Is this from A, B, or C from above? No. This is from the preamble to the 1952 GOP platform. It is, arguably, a more classically liberal document than the Democrats, and in it one can certainly perceive the coming "conservative" resurgence (Goldwater and Reagan) in such phrases as this: "We charge that they [the Democratic governments of FDR and Truman] have arrogantly deprived our citizens of precious liberties by seizing powers never granted."

Indeed, to a contemporary, classically liberal conservative, the 1952 Republican credo is actually quite inspiring in its muscular assertiveness about America's founding principles.* (It is, however, interesting to note that the Republicans endorsed a "Constitutional Amendment providing equal rights for men and women" and equal pay for equal work.) But the point of all this ought to be obvious: Whereas there are significant policy differences evident in the two major-party platforms, there is a remarkable unity on matters of *premise*. Both are patriotic and anti-totalitarian; both champion strong national defense; both reaffirm limited government—even if the Democrats hedge their commitment and the Republicans overstate theirs.

Jump ahead eight years, and in the lead-up to the race between John F. Kennedy and Richard M. Nixon, the Democrats' platform begins with another powerful statement of principle:

> Our objective . . . is not the right to coexist in armed camps on the same planet with totalitarian ideologies; it is the creation of an enduring peace in which the universal values of human dignity, truth, and justice under law are finally secured for all men everywhere on earth.
>
> If America is to work effectively for such a peace, we must first restore our national strength—military, political, economic, and moral.

Echoes, it seems to me, of George W. Bush.

---

*There are some remarkable inclusions that remind us how far we have come since 1952, such as this from the GOP's statement on Civil Rights: "We will prove our good faith by . . . [taking] Federal action toward the elimination of lynching."

Needless to say, both the Democratic and Republican platforms of 1960 are strongly anticommunist, although the GOP
statement is the more powerful:

> The leadership of the United States must be responsible and
> mature; its promises must be rational and practical, soberly
> pledged and faithfully undertaken. Its purposes and its aspi-
> rations must ascend to that high ground of right and free-
> dom upon which mankind may dwell and progress in decent
> security.

One might wish George W. Bush had read this in 2000.

The GOP platform is not predictive of future Republican policies toward China, and the Democrats' credo eerily suggests the
coming Bay of Pigs disaster, but—again—one senses that the two
parties were fully capable of carrying on a civil conversation, because they shared the same fundamental beliefs, shared the same
ambitious dreams.

Party platforms are not the only measure of the political temper of a time, but they are good ones—despite their partisan differences, as in, for instance, the two parties' views of the state of
the economy of 1960: dreadful, said the Dems; buoyant, said the
Reps. But when American men and women sit down to discuss
their views about the nation, evoking its past and in consideration
of its future, they necessarily conjure—or *used* to—the spirit of
the Founders, and hope to capture some of the wisdom and common sense that characterized the thought and action of such great
men on behalf of so great a people as we American are and deserve to be. It's notable that the 1960 GOP platform ends on a

note of conciliation—at a time, recall, when the party had been in power for eight years and had every reason to suppose it would be for the next four. "[W]e have tried to refrain from writing a merely partisan document. We have no wish to exaggerate differences between ourselves and the Democratic Party. . . ." To be sure, the statement goes on to discuss such differences, although not with exaggeration. The difference cited hardly seemed fundamental then; it may be now. But the Republicans presented them simply as facts and not as an indictment:

> There are many things a free government cannot do for its people as well as they can do them for themselves. There are some things no government should promise or attempt to do. The functions of government are so great as to bear no needless enlargement. We limit our proposals and our pledges to those areas for which the government of a great republic can reasonably be made responsible. To the best of our ability we have avoided advocating measures that would go against the grain of a free people.

The Democrats began by discussing Thomas Jefferson. The Republicans ended by evoking him: *That government governs best that governs least.**

It's clear that in the past the members of the two political parties have been able to speak with civility to one another. There have, of course, been moments when that civility has broken down, most notably when in 1856 Charles Sumner of Massachu-

---

*Again, it may be that this quote, usually attributed to Jefferson, is not actually a direct quote but more a summary of the man's clear belief with regard to government.

setts gave an antislavery speech on the Senate floor in which he denounced the Kansas-Nebraska Act, verbally assaulted Stephen Douglas of Illinois as a "noise-some, squat, and nameless animal," and ridiculed the speech defect of Andrew Butler of South Carolina. Two days later, Preston Brooks, a congressman and nephew of Butler, nearly beat Sumner to death with a walking stick. The incident was both a portent of the Civil War that was to come and perhaps even a cause of the war, in that the Brooks attack is thought to have propelled the growth of the Republican Party, the end of compromise on the slavery issue, and the rise to prominence of Abraham Lincoln.

The Smears We Cannot Abide

By now the reader may have surmised that the author believes America's future depends upon citizens who are genuinely patriotic, largely sympathetic to our military, religious or tolerant of religious faith, and cognizant of the virtues of competitive enterprise. From this it follows that the nation will suffer as these fundamental aspects of American life are smeared by the Left.

In truth, it's hard to know how much America's future is put at risk by the inexorable attacks upon patriotism, soldering, faith, and capitalism. I fear that the status of these institutions and values is being diminished in the popular imagination and that consequently ground is being ceded to leftist policy innovations that may one day have the effect of making America unrecognizable in terms of the traditions that have made the nation great.

I fear this, but on the other hand I have faith in the American people—faith that we love our country, are willing to fight for our country, believe deeply in Providence, and understand the viability and virtue of free markets. Recent world history has shown the utter futility of the kind of statist policies advocated by left-liberals, and recent American history has shown that, whereas the Democratic Party may be momentarily ascendant and may be the uneasy political home of the Left, the American people may be expected to punish liberals—at the ballot box—if the trend in politics and society moves leftward.

Many leftists in our universities—and those they influence in the media and in public life—believe that smears and other lies are appropriate because, in the words of one of the contemporary Left's leading lights, the late French philosopher Michel Foucault: "There are no facts."

It remains to be seen how many Americans will come to believe the same. For now, let me simply summarize why the liberal campaign to defame America must not succeed.

Defending Patriots

The scourge of patriotism is multiculturalism and its evil twin political correctness, which poet David Lehman has called "the euphemism made instinctive":

> It is the systematic substitution of wish-fulfillment for reality. The U.S. Postal Service issues a commemorative stamp honoring the painter Jackson Pollock but airbrushes out the cigarette in the famous photo of him. The aim is to stamp out cigarettes, and perhaps it is a worthy aim, but the erasure not only bullies the populace but dishonors the truth, Pollock's truth, which is that he was not only a great painter but also a highly volatile, hard-drinking chain-smoker hell-bent on self-destruction.[16]

We've seen how Left elites will, in the service of their notions of what's best for the rest, impose their will. (Think of New York's City Council.) They can't be patriotic, because they believe that American history is all about oppression, and because they think the people (Republican voters anyhow) are ignorant. In the words of novelist Jane Smiley: "Ignorance and bloodlust have a long tradition in the United States, especially in the red states." Honestly, if that were true, we might all question patriotism.

Smiley—and what a wonderful name for such a frowning lady—manages to smear just about everybody. But then, in her defense, she was pretty upset by the 2004 presidential election:

> A generation ago, the big capitalists, who have no morals, as we know, decided to make use of the religious right in their class war against the middle class and against the regulations that were protecting those whom they considered to be their rightful prey—workers and consumers. The architects of this strategy knew perfectly well that they were exploiting, among other unsavory qualities, a long American habit of virulent racism, but they did it anyway, and we see the outcome now—Cheney is the capitalist arm and Bush is the religious arm. They know no boundaries or rules. They are predatory and resentful, amoral, avaricious, and arrogant. Lots of Americans like and admire them because lots of Americans, even those who don't share those same qualities, don't know which end is up. Can the Democrats appeal to such voters? Do they want to? The Republicans have sold their souls for power. Must everyone?[17]

The implications of such an attitude, in terms of policy prescription, are pretty far from what we'd consider the American center. And her views are quite typical of the Left, which is probably why, in the aftermath of 9/11, one university student shyly asked his history professor, "Would it be okay now for us to be patriotic?" The student was fortunate: the professor said yes.[18]

But let the last word on patriotism come from David McCullough: "Keep in mind," he once told an interviewer, "that patriotism means love of country, and that concept has held true."

> Those who have served this country have been willing to give up more than they gained. They have had no idea how things would turn out. The men who signed the Declaration knew they were declaring themselves as traitors to England and would be hung if they were caught.
>
> And, yes, we still sustain that kind of patriotism. Disagreement and dissonance, rivalry, bad feelings among people in positions of political leadership have been here from the beginning. It was true then, and it's true now.[19]

Defending Soldiers

Here's a paradox: These days, when people call for a draft or assert the need for universal military service—as nations as different as Israel and Switzerland require*—it is almost always intended as a kind of blow struck for pacifism. Writing for the liberal *American Prospect* online, David L. Englin gave a sensible expression of this notion:

---

*Armstrong Williams has written: "Mandatory military service is one of the oldest forms of national service and is common to both democratic and non-democratic countries. Such democratic countries as Austria, Brazil, Denmark, Finland, Germany, Israel, Mexico, Norway, Russia, South Korea, Sweden, Switzerland and Turkey require male and occasionally female citizens to participate in military service when they become 18 years old" (*Newsmax*, June 19, 2006).

How different our national discussion about preemptive war with Iraq would be if people had to look into the eyes of their own sons and daughters and decide whether their lives were worth risking. But with fewer than half of 1 percent of Americans serving in the military (and that's after the post-September 11 mobilization of the National Guard and Reserve forces), the number of Americans even acquainted with, let alone related to, a serviceman or woman is at a modern low.[20]

I have no quarrel with that statement, except to note that the All-Volunteer Force has been so effective that there is currently no sentiment at any level of government to change it—except among those with pacifist intentions. Englin goes on to note that such a solution to military adventures he and others deem inappropriate "may sound harsh, but . . . personalizing the burdens of war would harness democracy to ensure that any particular war is truly necessary—truly a matter of action being less costly and more moral than inaction." But this is specious. How does making war a matter of public opinion (or as Englin puts it, transforming "the decision to go to war from a cost-free intellectual analysis into an appropriately grave choice with intimate personal consequences") guarantee that the decision to fight would be ipso facto necessary? This has the unsettling subtext—as does so much superficially reasonable leftist writing—of building into American military service something like treason.

The press has lately made common cause with dissident members of America's intelligence services to publicize military secrets, but—beyond those betrayals of mission—we must acknowledge that there are sound reasons why the President, and others engaged in exercising the nation's military might, needs to make the case for such actions to the American people. But there will always be—must always be—a cloud of uncertainty about the nature of threats, unless we wish to let America's enemies know exactly what we know about them. The idea that the soldiers themselves might cherry-pick engagements into which they are deployed is mindboggling. "Universal military service," Englin claims, "would also strengthen our social fabric by bringing the reality of America closer to America's ideals," but whose ideals? Doesn't he mean the antiwar Left? To be fair, he has many good things to say about the military experience, though most have to do with democratizing American life. None has to do with fulfilling the military's mission, which is protecting the nation by killing our enemies.

> Forcing families across America to share in the "wounds and scars of war" through universal military service would not be a recipe for a pacifist United States. How many Americans would have avoided taking on al-Qaeda and its Taliban protectors for fear of risking the safety of a friend or a loved one?[21]

That was written in 2002, and we now know that the answer is that lots of Americans have avoided taking on al Qaeda and the Taliban—and more every day wish not to as the war's progress founders. There are sad, problematic, and even dire consequences, but what might the current situation be were the fighting force composed of sunshine warriors?

We met Rep. Charles Rangel in Chapter 3 in the context of his comments to the effect that military recruits are disproportionately poor and poorly educated. Rangel has called for universal military because he believes it will prevent military action. "I think, if we went home and found out that there were families concerned about their kids going off to war," he told CNN, "there would be more cautiousness and more willingness to work with the international community than to say, 'Our way or the highway.'" Pretty clearly, his goal isn't patriotic service to one's nation, but some extra-political means of affecting defense policy. And this view has surprisingly widespread appeal—to liberals, to some isolationist conservatives, and to antistatist libertarians.* It may be that America's status as a large, powerful, and geographically isolated country may mean we would be relatively safe with a "democratic" military essentially unwilling to fight except against masses of invaders, a condition (survival of the homeland) that even the above-named groups would endorse. But under such conditions this would also surely mean America would not have joined the fight in World War II. Why? Because the Japanese, knowing this "universal" and "democratic" character of the America's military, would not have attacked Pearl Harbor. Certainly, America would almost surely not have declared war against

---

*Mind you, an argument can certainly be made for mandatory military service. Consider this: "The United States benefits from conscription because national spirit increases, national unity improves, neighborhoods become safer, and society grows healthier. With conscription, troubled teens who normally head to street corners enter the military and receive the training, discipline and experience that propel them to a stable and secure life. They unite with people of all sexes, races and religions to work toward a common good. This allows neighborhoods to become safer and society to become stronger. The workforce gets better workers, families get better mothers and fathers, and the country gets a more unified citizenship." (Armstrong Williams, cited in an earlier footnote.) That's alluring, but the flaw of the argument is its assumption that the armed forces ought to primarily serve other social ends than its military mission.

Nazi Germany. Perhaps America's World War II would simply have been a Pacific war, unless German U-boats began to prey on American ships wherever they found them.

More specifically with regard to our current crisis, we can see the effect the Left is having on the course of the war on terror. As I write this, both houses of Congress have passed one or another version of "nonbinding" bills to withhold war funding and withdraw troops from Iraq. To be sure, much in the conduct of the war has not gone well, but it's fair to ask if we are coming to a point at which fighting itself—anywhere in the world and for any reason—is being taken off the table. Scholar Karl Zinsmeister writes:

> Military education is not especially complicated. It is based on a few very clear, very settled, very stern principles. In a fuzzy, lazy, sold-out time, the military code is crisp, demanding, and uncompromised. In an era willing to sanction anything, good military education teaches young people to be intolerant: of disloyalty, half-heartedness, injustice, and cowardice. Many of the young Americans who enter military education today have never encountered such ideas before.
>
> The military ethic is in many ways an antidote to the lolling libertinism of modern life. Whether this throwback code can retain its essential stiffness in the face of today's cultural breezes remains to be seen, but there are signs that a large and hungry market still exists for these ancient, time-tested verities. Anyone who has watched some purposeless Gen X child drift into Parris Island, only to march home as an honor-bound man and Marine (and that continues to happen every day in this country) can see firsthand that many

young Americans are crying out for the clear limits and elevated ideals that martial life teaches.[22]

I've gone on at some length here, because, as I said at the start of this book, we may be able to survive without patriotism, faith, and economic liberty but never without our soldiers, Marines, sailors, and airmen.

Defending the Faithful

Thinking again about the Declaration of Independence—and thinking of the Declaration as the premier statement of fundamental Americanism—we recognize something marvelous in the Founders' vision of us. Our rights are God-given. They don't come from legislators or presidents or philosophers or professors; they don't even spring from our own rich history and tradition. We are endowed by our Creator with the rights to the good things in life, not least of which—indeed the greatest of which—is liberty.

Attacks on religion and on believers by the Left go to the heart of leftist thinking. If, as Monsieur Foucault had it, there really are no facts, it's principally because there is no God. Whereas if, in fact, God exists, then we are full-freighted with facts and other burdens such as responsibilities and duties, which have no power if they are thought up on the spur of the moment by a professor of philosophy at Berkeley or Harvard.

I happen to be Catholic, and back in the eighties and nineties I recall the brouhaha about abortion and Catholic politicians in New York that pitted John J. O'Connor, archbishop of New York, against Gov. Mario Cuomo and Democratic vice-presidential nominee Geraldine Ferraro—and then spread across the nation.

(The same issue was very much in play during the 2004 campaign, with some clerics indicating they would refuse communion to John Kerry because of his advocacy of abortion rights, which clearly contradicts the teaching of the Catholic Church, of which Sen. Kerry is a communicant.) David Boldt, the editor of the *Philadelphia Inquirer*, wrote that

> [The bishops'] efforts reflect a lack of understanding as to just how delicate the balance between church and state is. . . . The Roman Catholic Church, it needs to be remembered, is quite literally an unAmerican institution. It is not democratic. The church's views on due process and on the status of women, to name just a couple of key issues, are sharply at odds with those that inform the laws of American secular society. And its principal policies are established by the Vatican in Rome.[23]

This reminded me of the joke I heard as a kid after John F. Kennedy was inaugurated: Did you hear that JFK broke his leg at the White House? Yeah, he broke it when he tripped over the Pope's bags.

William F. Buckley could only shake his head:

> The first point to make here is that every religion is un-American if it is conceded that Mr. Boldt used that term correctly. The trouble with "un-American" is that it suggests anti-American, as in, the House Committee on Un-American Activities. But of course it would be difficult to make that point convincingly given that the gentlemen who stitched this country together were almost all of them reli-

giously committed folk, so that the term "extra-American" suggests itself, if you are looking for a word that acknowledges another authority than that of Congress and the courts to govern your behavior.[24]

And, as Buckley concludes, since our Founders were themselves religious, and since they sought vigorously to protect religious freedom, it's actually un-American to suggest that proclaiming faith in the public square is . . . un-American.

"If our Founding Fathers' sole intent [in the First Amendment's Establishment Clause] was to delete God and prayer from" public life, writes Donna R. LaPlante in *New Oxford Review*,

> [T]hey would not have lavished Washington, D.C., with religious paintings, statues of religious figures, Scripture quotes referencing God, and numerous displays of the Ten Commandments. Nor did they consider saying a prayer at the beginning of each session in the House and Senate a violation of the freedom they sought to establish and protect. James Madison underscored the importance of Christian values to our nation's founding when he said, "We stake the future of this country on our ability to govern ourselves under the principles contained in the Ten Commandments." Our civic ancestors did not think that including God in their daily pursuits as public figures or as private citizens was wrong or politically incorrect; they simply considered it the exercise of their newfound freedom to do so. Apparently, our Founding Fathers and early statesman did not interpret the First Amendment in quite the same way as our present-day liberal judges.[25]

Defending the Entrepreneur

In 1996, the *New York Times* ran a seven-part series of articles about the economy called "The Downsizing of America" that may represent the high point of the Left's anticapitalist smear campaign. The series claimed to prove that there was something un-American about job loss that resulted from the normal character of free enterprise.*

But the *Washington Post's* economics writer, Robert J. Samuelson, begged to differ. "Good reporting is fact-finding without prejudice," he wrote. "You go where the evidence leads. But the *Times'* 'reporting' was of an inferior type. It involved the selective collection of information to buttress what editors and reporters had already concluded."[26]

In 1944, the future Nobel Laureate Friedrich Hayek wrote a book called *The Road to Serfdom* about the challenges to liberty from various forms of collectivism, hard (communism, socialism) and soft (welfarism and interventionism):

> Our generation has forgotten that the system of private property is the most important guaranty of freedom. It is only because the control of the means of production is divided among many people acting independently that we as individuals can decide what to do with ourselves. When all the means of production are vested in a single hand, whether

---

*The economist Joseph Schumpeter used the term "creative destructiveness" to describe the way the innovations of capitalism upset the established order. It is said (I recall the story from George Gilder's book *Wealth and Poverty* [Basic Books, 1981]) that Henry Bessemer, the developer of the process for making steel, stood on a hillside looking down at iron works and said, "Today, I've destroyed all of this."

it be nominally that of "society" as a whole or that of a dictator, whoever exercises this control has complete power over
us. In the hands of private individuals, what is called economic power can be an instrument of coercion, but it is never
control over the whole life of a person. But when economic
power is centralized as an instrument of political power it
creates a degree of dependence scarcely distinguishable from
slavery. It has been well said that, in a country where the sole
employer is the state, opposition means death by slow star-
vation.[27]

And, of course, all these matters are related. "Capitalism is utterly dependent on the Judeo-Christian tradition," Rabbi Daniel
Lapin has said. "No capital market has ever grown indigenously
outside of Christendom. It's not a coincidence that atheistic regimes have proven incapable of running viable economies."[28]

Johan Norberg, the Danish scientist who has taken so much
heat for his counterintuitive views about climate change, expressed
as well as anyone the debt we owe to the people who take risks to
make money:

> The people we should thank are the innovators and entre-
> preneurs, the individuals who see new opportunities and risk
> exploring them—the people who find new markets, create
> new products, think out new ways to handle commodities
> commercially, organize work in new ways, design new tech-
> nology or transfer capital to more productive uses. The en-
> trepreneur is an explorer, who ventures into uncharted
> territory and opens up the new routes along which we will
> all be traveling soon enough. Simply to look around is to

understand that entrepreneurs have filled our lives with everyday miracles.[29]

But he knows we should never expect the Left to offer thanks.
For them there are only victims—and only answers that come
from an imperious elite, mandating a form of justice that has no
relation to liberty.

The Left's Big-Government Mistake

The Left's desire to defy the gravity of the republican principle of
government restraint is actually self-defeating. Every time the national government is empowered to enter a new sphere of American life on behalf of some "liberal" cause, it is empowered, *period*.
This means that when power shifts and the Right gains control of
the mechanisms of government it will as enthusiastically impose
its policies with the force of law as did the Left when it had its
day. This is why many conservative activists and voters abandoned
the GOP in 2006—a boon to Democrats and liberals that will
almost surely be short-lived.

I believe this cycle of alternating versions of Big Government
is the result of the activist policies in Washington that had their
heyday in the period between the New Deal and the Vietnam
War. By 1976, the decline of the appeal of Big Government was
under way, culminating in the elections of "reform" candidates to
the presidency: Ronald Reagan, who very specifically campaigned
as a champion of privatization and devolution; George H. W.
Bush, who was Reagan's epigone; Bill Clinton, who *seemed* enam-
ored of smaller government and of "ending welfare as we know
it"; and George W. Bush, whose "compassionate conservatism"

gave promise of even more decentralization. Meanwhile, each of them actually expanded the powers of government in their attempts to achieve particular ends, with the result that Washington is still the center of America's governmental universe, with its moonlike pull on the tides of everyday life growing ever stronger. This is simply no good for anybody. If politics really is simply a matter of power—of manipulating the mechanisms of society in such a way as to achieve the ideological ends one seeks, and if one consequence of this is—and it certainly is—an empowered government, what happens in the cycles of politics when your opponents get their shot at control? One of the greater ironies of recent history has been the extent to which liberals have become positively apoplectic about George W. Bush and his power, when—really—the basis of his power has been the liberal project of enhancing the breadth and depth of federal authority.

Add to this seemingly inexorable trend, the rise of the multicultural ideal and its fundamentally un-American content. (The only thing American about it is a sense of fair play for all.) The effect of multiculturalism has been to equalize the principles of the American founding with any and every other principle no matter what its genesis, but with special emphasis on the ethos and ideals of failed societies, whether Marxism or Mexico. As liberal historian Arthur Schlesinger Jr. once quipped about the essence of multiculturalism: *Too much pluribus, not enough unum.*

Multiculturalism is a stick with which the elites in media and the universities attempt to beat back American tradition and bypass the democratically expressed will of the people. The terrible thing about these Mandarins is they do not love the people; they do not respect the people; they do not trust the people.

The Founders worried about factions, and they were right to

do so. I'm not sure they worried about apathy, but they might have. This is especially so when the cause of the apathy is a kind of nihilism. Or at least I think it is.

Some months ago, with our older son away at school (West Point) and our younger son away on a church work trip (in Puerto Rico), my wife and I got a preview of our fast-approaching empty nest, and took the occasion to visit some of New York City's newer and better restaurants, a couple of which were in the area of Greenwich Village and New York University. As we walked around in the area of Washington Square Park, I was struck by the demeanor of the young people there, many of them NYU students. Having been in college in the sixties and seventies, I am familiar with and hardly offended by the sight of sloppiness and the remarkable conformity of style that always accompanies the contemporary sense of what is cool. What I wasn't really prepared for was the number of kids who were wearing surplus military garb (and various items in camouflage pattern), which I suppose they purchased a little farther uptown at Cheap Jack's or another of the local thrift stores. Ever since the sixties and the Vietnam War, this ironic adornment has been popular among antiwar types, I suppose because it sends a message of perverse militancy.

Because I'm a sort of inveterate convert (to Catholicism and conservatism), I've mostly been free of the fuddy-duddy verbiage of conservatism: the get-a-job, get-a-haircut quips I used to hear when I was twenty with hair down to my shoulders. But looking at the kids in Washington Square, I felt old and angry at their tattooed and buttoned indifference to the service and sacrifice being given for them by other young men and women, the ones in Iraq and Afghanistan. I don't begrudge the neo-hippies their right of political protest, but I was galled—I am galled—by their assumption (or what I took to be their assumption) that America requires nothing of them except their indifference and contempt. Time was when the cri de coeur of William Butler Yeats ("The Second Coming") was that: "The best lack all conviction, while the worst/ Are full of passionate intensity." But I couldn't detect a shred of passion among the students at NYU, although lack of conviction seemed to be in abundance.

I know, of course, that this is a bit of glib reductionism with regard to a large and complex Manhattan neighborhood, and that there are conservative students and committed students and in numbers that might be impressive, though I doubt that last part. But about one thing I'm sure: these kids and so many others are being encouraged to reject the very institutions and ideals that have given them the liberty to reject those institutions and ideals.

Patriotism, war, faith, and enterprise cannot be rejected— either through the embrace of internationalism, pacifism, atheism, and socialism or simply through indifference. Without men and women who love America, who are willing and able to fight and die for liberty, who pray for peace and remember the true source of our rights, and who let freedom thrive in the marketplace, not only will America be diminished, it won't be America anymore. It may more resemble a nation as conceived of by Michael Moore, one reflecting the principles embodied in his latest documentary film, *SiCKO*, in which—among other points made in condemnation of the nation's health-care system—Moore takes a group of ailing people to Cuba to receive free treatment. Free!

Cuba, of course, is run by Fidel Castro, who has been in power in Havana since 1959. He is a dictator—with all the attendant brutality that term implies. Is this really what the Left wants? To see American led by our own version of "El Jefe"? Short answer:

YES. Despite the fact that Castro had had Cuba under his thumb for nearly half a century, liberals don't care, because they think he's the *smartest* Cuban. Of course it helps that he is also anti-American, but what they really admire is the notion that Fidel is more competent than everybody else on his island fiefdom. God help us if the popularity of *SiCKO* actually convinces Americans there is any truth to that.

> Truthful lips endure forever, but a lying tongue lasts only a moment.
>
> —PROVERBS 12:19

ACKNOWLEDGMENTS

This book was the brainchild of my agent and friend, Alexander C. Hoyt. Still, we can't blame him for the result.

Alex managed to convince Calvert Morgan at HarperCollins that *Smear Tactics* was a worthy project, and if this book is less than perfect, it isn't because Cal didn't make his best efforts to set it right.

Linda Bridges read the first draft and made many, many fine suggestions for improving it.

My former colleagues at Bookspan/Doubleday Entertainment have been generous to me in many ways, not least in allowing me some flextime during the last months of writing *Smear Tactics*.

My wife, Sydny, and my older son, Robert, continually inspire me. Syd especially knows what a struggle it is to write and what a short-tempered lout I can be when the battle seems all uphill.

Finally, I owe a great deal indeed to my younger son, Jonathan, who was my research assistant on this book. I hope Jon learned a thing or two about the rough-and-tumble of American politics. He saved me countless hours of time, and he was a marvelous sounding board for the ideas that ended up in the book. What a pleasure for a father to have such sons.

NOTES

Chapter 1

1. Quoted in David McCullough, *John Adams* (New York: Simon & Schuster, 2001).
2. www.redcross.org/news/ds/hurricanes/2005/index.html.
3. NOAA's predictions reflect "a continuation of above-normal activity that began in 1995, and will likely be the seventh extremely active season since 1995," www.cpc.ncep.noaa.gov/products/outlooks/hurricane.shtml.
4. www.sourcewatch.org/index.php?title=George_W._Bush:_Hurricane _Katrina.
5. www.michaelmoore.com/words/message/index.php?id=183.
6. Philippe Grangereau, quoted in William F. Buckley Jr., "Is Bush a Racist?" www.nationalreview.com/buckley/wfb200509131545.asp.
7. http://newsbusters.org/node/841.
8. David Gonzalez, "Storm and Crisis," *New York Times*, September 2, 2005.
9. Ibid.
10. Quoted at littlegreenfootballs.com, entry 17326.
11. www.mirror.co.uk/news/tm_objectid=15938967&method=full&siteid =94762&headline=so-many-of-the-people-here-were-underprivileged -anyway-so-this-is-working-very-well-for-them-name_page.html.
12. Ward Churchill, "Some People Push Back: On the Justice of Roasting Chickens," *Pockets of Resistance* #11, September 2001.

13. Nancy Giles, "What If They Were White?" *CBS Sunday Morning,* September 4, 2005, www.cbsnews.com/stories/2005/09/04/sunday/main814720.shtml.

14. Ben Stein, "A Big Lie Put to Rest," The American Spectator Online, September 27, 2005.

15. Deroy Murdock, "Grand Wizard Bush," National Review Online, October 5, 2005.

16. Mark Steyn, "Media Deserve Blame for New Orleans Debacle," *Chicago Sun Times*, October 2, 2005.

17. Http://confederateyankee.mu.nu/archives/161432.php.

18. "Debunking the Myths of Katrina," *Popular Mechanics,* March 2006.

19. http://blackrod.blogspot.com/2005/09/happy-anniversary-buckhead-rathergate.html.

20. Michael Grunwald, "Money Flowed to Questionable Projects," *Washington Post,* September 8, 2005.

21. www.foxnews.com/story/0,2933,168105,00.html.

22. Robert F. Kennedy Jr., "For They That Sow the Wind Shall Reap the Whirlwind," www.huffingtonpost.com, August 29, 2005.

23. Ross Gelbspan, "Katrina's Real Name," *Boston Globe*, August 25, 2005.

24. Susan Jones, "Liberal Group Lays Out Its Agenda," www.cnsnews.com, September 22, 2005.

25. Patrick J. Michaels, S. Fred Singer, and David H. Douglas, "Settling Global Warming Science," Tech Central Station, August 12, 2004.

26. Tim Ball, "Coalition of the Seething," Tech Central Station, September 16, 2005.

27. www.yale.edu/envrocenter/yale_epoll2007_topline.pdf.

28. http://opinionjournal.com/best/?id=110009865.

29. www.whoi.edu/institutes/occi/viewArticle.do?id=10046.

30. Thomas Sowell, "Global Hot Air," National Review Online, February 13, 2007.

31. Michael Fumento, "Media Lied, People Died," Tech Central Station, October 14, 2005.

32. www.huffingtonpost.com/randall-robinson/new-orleans_b_6643.html.

33. Ibid.

34. "Debunking the Myths of Katrina," *Popular Mechanics*, March 2006.

35. www.dailykos.com/story/2005/8/31/163230/120.

36. Mort Kondracke, "Democrats Lead By Miles in 2004 'Smear' Campaigns," RealClearPolitics.com, March 2, 2004.

37. Nancy McPhee, *The Book of Insults* (New York: St. Martin's Press, 1978).

38. Philip Dray, *Stealing God's Thunder: Benjamin Franklin's Lightning Rod and the Invention of America* (New York: Random House, 2005).

39. Eric Burns, *Infamous Scribblers: The Founding Fathers and the Rowdy Beginnings of American Journalism* (New York: Public Affairs, 2006), pp. 58-59.

40. Lawrence Farmer, MD, "When Cotton Mather Fought the Smallpox" in *American Heritage*, August 1957, reprinted online: www.american heritage.com/articles/magazine/ah/1957/5/1957_5_40.shtml).

41. www.pbs.org/wgbh/amex/adams/peopleevents/p_callender.html.

42. Op. cit., McPhee.

43. www.monticello.org/plantation/hemingscontro/hemings-jefferson_con tro.html.

44. http://en.wikipedia.org/wiki/Sally_Hemings.

45. www.jewishworldreview.com/cols/chavez010406.asp.

46. www.usnews.com/usnews/opinion/articles/051024/24barone.htm.

47. Sowell, Thomas, *A Conflict of Visions: Ideological Origins of Political Conflict* (New York: Basic Books, 2002), p. 25.

48. Ibid., p. 40.

49. Ibid., pp. 59-60.

50. Edmund Burke, *Reflections on the Revolution in France*, vol. II of *Select Works of Edmund Burke: A New Imprint of the Payne Edition* (Indianap-olis, Ind.: Liberty Fund, 1999).

51. David Lebedoff, *The Uncivil War: How a New Elite Is Destroying Our Democracy* (Lanham, Md.: Taylor, 2004), p. 107.

52. Jonah Goldberg, "Bush = Hitler," National Review Online, September 4, 2003, www.nationalreview.com/goldberg/goldberg090403.asp.

53. Dwayne Wickham, "Boondocks' comic echoes African-American thoughts," *USA Today*, October 21, 2002.

54. Harvey Wasserman, "Bush's 9/11 Reichstag Fire," *Columbus Free Press*, September 12, 2002.

55. www.newsmax.com/archives/ic/2005/6/8/124621.shtml.

56. www.popularmechanics.com/blogs/911myths/4213805.html.

57. www.mrc.org/Profiles/odonnell/welcome.asp.

58. http://rasmussenreports.com/public_content/politics/22_believe_bus_ knew_about_9_11_attacks_in_advance.

Chapter 2

1. "Put Out No Flags," *The Nation*, October 8, 2001.
2. Quoted at www.rasmusen.org/w/04.05.17a.htm.
3. David Smyth, "Pop-star Chicks Turn Country on Its Head," *Evening Standard* (London), March 11, 2003.
4. Associated Press, March 14, 2003.
5. Adam Sweeting, "How the Chicks Survived Their Scrap with Bush," *The Telegraph*, June 15, 2006.
6. Adlai Stevenson, speech to the American Legion Convention in New York City, August 27, 1952.
7. Op. cit., Burke, *Reflections on the Revolution in France*.
8. James Burnham, "Sock It to Us, Herbert," *National Review*, November 19, 1968.
9. Noam Chomsky, *American Power and the New Mandarins* (New York: Pantheon, 1969).
10. Lawrence Auster, "The Regents' Round Table," *National Review*, December 8, 1989.
11. *National Review*, October 1, 2001.
12. www.politicalgateway.com/news/read.html?id=2739.
13. http://cndyorks.gn.apc.org/news/articles/talkofthetown.htm.
14. Morgan Reynolds, "Why Did the Trade Center Skyscrapers Collapse?" www.lewrockwell.com/reynolds/reynolds12.html.
15. Richard Stanley and Jerry Russell, "The Five-Sided Fantasy Island," www.911-strike.com/pentagon.htm.
16. www.flight93crash.com.
17. Maria Newman, "Poet Laureate Stands by Words Against Israel and Won't Step Down," *New York Times*, October 3, 2002.
18. www.campus-watch.org/article/id/853.
19. www.duke.edu/web/forums/cooke.html.
20. www.caribbeannetnews.com/cgi-script/csArticles/articles/000049/004979.htm.
21. http://hughhewitt.com/archives/2006/01/22-week/index.php#a001126.
22. Ann Coulter, *Godless: The Church of Liberalism* (New York: Crown Forum, 2006).
23. www.breitbart.com/news/2006/06/07/D8I3LT281.html.
24. www.newsmax.com/archives/ic/2006/6/8/101032.shtml.
25. www.opinionjournal.com/medialog/?id=110004950.

26. Susan Estrich, *Soulless: Ann Coulter and the Right-Wing Church of Hate* (New York: Regan, 2006).

27. Joe Maguire, *Brainless: The Lies and Lunacy of Ann Coulter* (New York: William Morrow, 2006).

28. Unanimous, *I Hate Ann Coulter!* (New York: Simon & Schuster, 2006).

29. Don Feder, "The Left's Dominionist Demons," FrontPageMagazine. com, May 5, 2005.

30. Wikipedia, "Breast Implants," http://en.wikipedia.org/wiki/Breast_implants.

31. Melik Kaylan, "Dr. Johnson, Meet Ann Coulter," *Wall Street Journal*, August 26, 2002.

32. Adam Nagourney, "G.O.P. Candidates Criticize Slur by Conservative Author," *New York Times*, March 4, 2007.

33. "An Open Letter . . ." at www.theamericanmind.com. The letter was signed by a number of noted bloggers and writers, including Sean Hackbarth, Kevin McCullough, Patrick Hynes, N. Z. Bear, and Glenn Reynolds.

34. Op. cit., Nagourney.

35. Anthony Summers, *Official and Confidential: The Secret Life of J. Edgar Hoover* (New York: Putnam, 1993).

36. Ronald Kessler, *The FBI: Inside the World's Most Powerful Law Enforcement Agency* (New York: Atria, 1993).

37. Michael Binyon, "US Was Main Target of Dirty Tricks," *The Times* (London), September 13, 1999.

38. Michelangelo Signorile, "Cardinal Spellman's Dark Legacy," *New York Press*, April 30, 2002.

39. William V. Shannon, "Guileless and Machiavellian," *New York Times*, October 28, 1984.

40. Nicholas von Hoffman, quoted in D'Souza, Dinesh, *Ronald Reagan: How an Ordinary Man Became an Extraordinary Leader* (Free Press, New York, 1977).

41. Ted Rall, "Reagan's Shameful Legacy: Mourn for Us, Not the Proto-Bush," commondreams.org, June 9, 2004.

42. Christopher Hitchens, "The Stupidity of Ronald Reagan," www.slate.com/id/2101842.

43. Irene Monroe, "Remembering Ronald Reagan's Evil Empire," www.thewitness.org/agw/monroe070804.html.

44. These SourceWatch quotes come from the site's entries for "smear" and

"evil empire," respectively:www.sourcewatch.org/index.php?title=Smear and www.sourcewatch.org/index.php?title=Evil_empire.

45. Joe Klein, "The Secrets of Reagan's Success," *Time*, June 6, 2004.

46. Ed Morrow, "Inventing Reagan," NationalReview.com, October 27, 2003.

47. Jim Rutenberg and Bill Carter, "CBS Is Said to Cancel Reagan Mini-Series," *New York Times*, November 4, 2003.

48. www.dynamist.com/weblog/archives/000627.html.

49. Op. cit., Rutenberg and Carter.

50. Bernard Weinraub, "CBS Is Reconsidering Mini-Series on Reagan," *New York Times*, November 4, 2003.

51. "CBS Cancels 'The Reagans,' " *New York Times*, November 5, 2003.

52. www.powerlineblog.com/archives/005021.php.

53. Paul Kengor, "Leftist Publishers Trash Reagan," FrontPage.com, February 20, 2007.

54. Kathleen Maclay, "Researchers help define what makes a political conservative," *UC Berkeley News*, July 22, 2003.

55. Ibid.

56. www.time.com/time/magazine/article/0,9171,838361,00.html.

57. Jonah Goldberg, "They Blinded Me with Science," National Review Online, July 24, 2003.

58. Scott Ott, "Medicare to Cover Conservatism Prevention Measures," ScappleFace.com, July 23, 2003.

59. Henry Fairlie, "Anti-Americanism at Home and Abroad," *Commentary*, December 1975.

60. Peregrine Worsthorne, quoted in Henry Fairlie, "Anti-Americanism at Home and Abroad."

61. "Johnny Depp: U.S. Is Like a Stupid Puppy," CNN.com, September 3, 2003.

62. http://news.bbc.co.uk/2/hi/entertainment/3083086.stm.

63. Victor Davis Hanson, "Loyalty, How Quaint," *National Review*, November 24, 2003.

64. www.codepinkalert.org/section.php?id=208.

65. "2004 Republican National Convention protest activity," Wikipedia, http://en.wikipedia.org/wiki/2004_Republican_National_Convention_protest_activity.

66. "Smearing the NYPD," *New York Post*, March 27, 2007.

67. www.boston.com/news/globe/editorial_opinion/oped/articles/2004/03/21/the_anatomy_of_a_smear_campaign/?page=2.

68. Byron York, "The Democratic Myth Machine," *National Review*, April 19, 2004.

69. www.cnn.com/2006/POLITICS/10/27/webb.allen/index.html.

70. Scott Galupo, "Allen's 'Lolita' Smear," *Washington Times*, October 27, 2006.

71. Cal Thomas, "The Truth Is, a Lie Helped Beat Virginia Senator," www.saukvalley.com/articles/2007/03/04/opinion/columnists/299930 127187845.prt.

72. Tim Craig and Michael D. Shear, "Webb Defends Novels Against Attacks," *Washington Post*, October 29, 2006.

Chapter 3

1. Elizabeth Weill-Greenberg, *10 Excellent Reasons Not to Join the Military* (New York: The New Press, 2006).

2. Bret Stephens, "Easongate," *Wall Street Journal*, February 10, 2005.

3. Howard Kurtz, "Eason Jordan, Quote, Unquote," *Washington Post*, February 8, 2005.

4. Reprinted at Jewish World Review, www.jewishworldreview.com/michelle/malkin020905.php3.

5. Byron York, "Bush and the National Guard," *National Review*, May 8, 2004.

6. www.foxnews.com/projects/pdf/091004_bush service.pdf.

7. http://powerlineblog.com/archives/007760.php.

8. http://powerlineblog.com/archives/009118.php.

9. www.usatoday.com/news/politicselections/nation/president/2004-09-21-cover-guard_x.htm.

10. http://daily.nysun.com/Repository/getmailfiles.asp?Style=OliveXLib: ArticleToMail&Type-text/html&Path=NYS/2004/09/21&ID=Ar0 0102.

11. www.captainsquartersblog.com/mt/archives/002575.php#.

12. www.foxnews.com/story/0,2933,132996,00.html.

13. www.freerepublic.com/focus/f-news/1221463/posts.

14. Mary Mapes, *Truth and Duty* (New York: St. Martin's Press, 2005).

15. www.transterrestrial.com/archives/005786.html.

16. www.iwf.org/inkwell/?archiveID=1014.

17. Donald P. Shaw and Zane E. Finkelstein, "Westmoreland vs. CBS," *Commentary*, August 1984.

18. Quoted by Professor Peter C. Rollins, "Behind the Westmoreland Trial of 1984," on www.vvi.org/Content/vvi2.asp.

19. Sally Bedell and Don Kowet, "Anatomy of a Smear," *TV Guide*, May 24, 1982.

20. Op. cit., Shaw and Finkelstein.

21. Op. cit., Rollins.
22. Lydia Saad, "Military Again Tops 'Confidence in Institutions' List," the Gallup Organization, June 1, 2005.
23. Op. cit., Weill-Greenberg.
24. http://education.military.com/money-for-school/use-it-or-lose-it.
25. Op. cit., Weill-Greenberg.
26. www.richmond.edu/~ebolt/history398/JohnKerryTestimony.html.
27. www.nationalreview.com/owens/owens200401270825.asp.
28. www.law.umkc.edu/faculty/projects/ftrials/mylai/Myl_hero.html#HU GH%20THOMPSON.
29. www.nationalreview.com/owens/owens200401270825.asp.
30. www.mediaresearch.org/BozellColumns/newscolumn/2004/col20040 824.asp.
31. www.emilitary.org/forums/index.php?s=9a00b5830aca4f15946f35cbe 6b9dfdf&showtopic=3609.
32. www.commondreams.org/views06/0124-23.htm.
33. "Swift Boat Smears," *Washington Post*, August 12, 2004.
34. "Media Reality Check" for Wednesday, August 18, 2004, www.mrc.org.
35. Mort Kondracke, "Democrats Lead By Miles in 2004 'Smear' Campaigns," RealClearPolitics.com, March 2, 2004.
36. *Wall Street Journal*, November 1, 2006, p. A18.
37. http://insider.washingtontimes.com/articles/normal. php?StoryID=20061031-093250-8735r.
38. "The Model of a Major Modern Democrat," Editorials, *New York Post*, November 2, 2006.
39. http://thebookblogger.com/compasspoints/2006/11/that_joke.html.
40. http://blog.thedemocraticdaily.com/?p=5880.
41. Josh Gerstein, "Rangel Adopts the Logic of Kerry's 'Joke'," *New York Sun,* November 27, 2006.
42. "Issues and Insights," Investor's Business Daily, May 31, 2005.
43. Rebecca Hagelin, "Trying to 'Rangel' Some Facts," Townhall.com, December 1, 2006.
44. Tim Kane, "Who Are the Recruits? The Demographic Characteristics of U.S. Military Enlistment, 2003-2005," www.heritage.org/Research/ NationalSecurity/cda06-09.cfm.
45. Ibid.
46. Quoted in W. Thomas Smith Jr., "One Democrat's Deception," National Review Online, November 29, 2006.
47. Quoted in James Taranto, "Responding to Rangel," Best of the Web, *Wall Street Journal*, November 28, 2006.

48. Ibid.
49. Richard Durbin, Wikipedia, http://en.wikipedia.org/wiki/Richard_Durbin.
50. Rowan A. Scarborough, "Gitmo Called Death Camp," *Washington Times*, June 16, 2005.
51. www.cnn.com/2005/POLITICS/06/21/guantanamo.durbin/.
52. Media Research Center, "Nets Target U.S. Military 'Abuses' But Skip Dick Durbin's 'Nazi' Rant," June 16, 2005.
53. www.mrc.org/printer/cyberalerts/2005/cyb20050610pf.asp.
54. *Editor & Publisher*, August 24, 2005.
55. Christopher Hitchens, "A War to Be Proud Of," *The Weekly Standard*, September 5, 2005.
56. www.brookesnews.com/062602mediabughraib.html.
57. www.freerepublic.com/focus/f-news/1145998/posts.
58. William J. Bennett, "Why We Fight," speech to the President's Club of the Claremont Institute, May 14, 2004.
59. "The Koranic Excesses," *Wall Street Journal*, June 6, 2005.
60. Quoted in Mark Steyn, "Quran Desecration Crock a Win for Jihad Spin Docs," *Chicago Sun-Times*, June 12, 2005.
61. William M. Arkin, "The Troops Also Need to Support the American People," *Washington Post*, January 30, 2007.
62. Ted Rall, April 29, 2004 in Ben Johnson, "The Left Smears an American Hero," FrontPageMagazine.com, May 24, 2004.
63. Maureen Dowd, "Why No Tea and Sympathy," *New York Times*, August 10, 2005.
64. www.truthout.org/cindy.shtml.
65. www.huffingtonpost.com/cindy-sheehan/friends-dont-let-friends_b_13163.html.
66. www.canada.com/topics/news/world/story.html?id=6b4e0fb3-7c4c-46f5-bf50-cf761780634a&k=60689.
67. Christopher Hitchens, "Cindy Sheehan's Sinister Piffle," www.slate.com/id/2124500/.
68. Peggy Noonan, "We're All Soldiers Now," *Wall Street Journal*, November 2, 2001.
69. James Q. Wilson, "The Press at War," *City Journal*, Autumn 2006.

Chapter 4

1. "The Real American Taliban," *New York Press*, January 2, 2002.
2. Patrick Hynes, *In Defense of the Religious Right* (Nashville, Tenn.: Nelson Current, 2006).
3. www.mediaresearch.org/cyberalerts/2004/cyb20041122.asp.
4. Michael Weisskopf, *Washington Post*, February 1, 1993. www.souljourners.org/links_view.php?record_id=3321
5. www.truthout.org/docs_2005/013105F.shtml.
6. www.worldnetdaily.com/news/article.asp?ARTICLE_ID=51956.
7. David Remnick, "The Wilderness Campaign," *The New Yorker*, September 13, 2004.
8. Op. cit., Hynes.
9. Ross Douthat, "Theocracy, Theocracy, Theocracy," in *First Things*, August/September 2006.
10. www.beliefnet.com/story/220/story_22000_1.html.
11. www.nytimes.com/2005/03/29/opinion/29krugman.html?ex=1269752400&en=861824859de01bcd&ei=5088&partner=rssnyt.
12. http://worldnetdaily.com/news/article.asp?ARTICLE_ID=40867.
13. www.washingtonpost.com/wp-dyn/content/article/2006/03/04/AR2006030401369.html.
14. www.damonlinker.com.
15. www.msnbc.msn.com/id/11769179/site/newsweek/.
16. Quoted by Leon Wieseltier, "The God Genome," *New York Times Book Review*, February 19, 2006.
17. www.usnews.com/usnews/news/articles/060417/17christ.htm.
18. www.buzzflash.com/interviews/06/02/int06006.html.
19. www.highbridgeaudio.com/thykingdomcome.html.
20. www.kingdomcoming.com/.
21. www.democracynow.org/article.pl?sid=07/02/19/1545218.
22. Op. cit., Douthat.
23. Kevin Phillips, *American Theocracy* (New York: Viking, 2006), p. vii.
24. Op. cit., Phillips, pp. viii-ix.
25. Ibid., p. 348.
26. John McCandlish Phillips, "When Columnists Cry 'Jihad'," *Washington Post*, May 4, 2005.
27. Maureen Dowd, "DeLay, Deny and Demagogue," *New York Times*, March 24, 2005.
28. Frank Rich, "The God Racket, from DeMille to DeLay," *New York Times*, March 27, 2005.

29. www.chalcedon.edu/credo.php.

30. E-mail exchange between Christopher Ortiz and the author, [MONTH?]2006.

31. Richard John Neuhaus, "Checks, Balances and Bishops," in The Public Square, *First Things*, August/September 2006.

32. www.firstthings.com/ftissues/ft0608/articles/ectstatement.html.

33. Mark Steyn, "Code Word: God Bless America," *Maclean's*, November 27, 2006.

34. www.salon.com/ent/feature/2006/08/01/mel/.

35. www.realclearpolitics.com/articles/2006/08/ jews_shot_in_seattle_left _angr.html.

36. Ibid.

37. www.washingtonpost.com/wp-dyn/content/article/2006/08/13/AR20 06081300906.html.

38. www.adl.org/Interfaith/gibson_qa.asp.

39. http://thebluestate.typepad.com/my_weblog/2006/07/mel_gibson_ jews.html.

40. www.foxnews.com/story/0,2933,220517,00.html.

41. www.huffingtonpost.com/bill-maher/the-world-is-mel-gibson_b_263 15.html.

42. Daniel C. Dennett, *Breaking the Spell* (New York: Penguin, 2006), p. 21.

43. Ibid., p. 327.

44. David B. Hart, "Daniel Dennett Hunts the Snark" *First Things,* January 2007.

Chapter 5

1. George Soros, "The Capitalist Threat," *Atlantic Monthly*, February 1997.

2. James Bartholomew, "We Need a Revision Course on Why Capitalism Is a Good Thing," *The Telegraph*, May 24, 2005.

3. Ibid.

4. Larry Ribstein, "Wall Street and Vine: Hollywood's View of Business," in Illinois Law and Economics Working Papers Series, Working Paper No. LE05-010.

5. Ibid.

6. www.businessandmedia.org/specialreports/2006/badcompanyII/badco mpanyII.asp.

7. Op. cit., Ribstein.

8. Kenneth Lloyd Billingsley, "Hollywood's Missing Movies," *Reason*, June 2000.

9. Quoted in Karl Zinsmeister, "Propaganda in America," *The American Enterprise*, May/June 1999.

10. www.imdb.com/title/tt0094291/quotes.

11. Lichter, Lichter and Rothman, quoted in Michael Fumento, "Why Hollywood Hates Business," *Investor's Business Daily*, January 3, 1992.

12. www.businessandmedia.org/specialreports/2006/badcompanyII/bad-companyII.asp.

13. *Star Trek: First Contact*, Paramount Pictures, 1996.

14. Rich Noyes, "A Summer of Skewed News: The Liberal Tilt in TV's Economic Reporting," Media Research Center, September 19, 2002.

15. www.acsh.org/healthissues/newsID.1427/healthissue_detail.asp.

16. Ibid.

17. Ibid.

18. www.foxnews.com/story/0,2933,63698,00.html.

19. Chuck Klosterman, "McDiculous," *Esquire*, May 2004.

20. Ibid.

21. James Glassman, "Dishing It Out, But Not Taking It," TCSDaily.com, May 27, 2004.

22. Ruth Kava, "A Supersized Distortion," TCSDaily.com, February 10, 2004.

23. www.techcentralstation.com/052704G.html.

24. www.nytimes.com/books/first/s/schlosser-fast.html?_r=1.

25. Bruce Fein, "Pull a Fast One," TCSDaily.com, March 11, 2003.

26. Thomas DiLorenzo, "Two Very Fashionable Frauds," Mises.org, October 20, 2004.

27. Craig Winneker, "A Whiff of Anti-Americanism," TCSDaily.com, May 30, 2006.

28. Ellen Goodman, "No Change in Political Climate," *Boston Globe*, February 9, 2007

29. Quoted by Michael O'Sullivan, *Washington Post*, June 2, 2006.

30. www.spiked-online.com/index.php?/site/article/1782/.

31. www.cbsnews.com/blogs/2006/03/22/publiceye/entry1431768.shtml.

32. Ian Sample, "Scientists Offered Cash to Dispute Climate Study," *The Guardian*, February 2, 2007.

33. Kenneth P. Green and Steven F. Hayward, "Scenes from the Climate Inquisition," *The Weekly Standard*, February 19, 2007.

34. Robert Samuelson, "Global Warming and Hot Air," *Washington Post*, February 7, 2007.

35. Op. cit., Green and Hayward.

36. Bjørn Lomborg, "Smearing a Skeptic," *Wall Street Journal*, January 23, 2003.
37. Ibid.
38. Ibid.
39. "The Ideological Environmentalist," *The New Atlantis*, Winter 2004.
40. Ibid.
41. Ibid.
42. Neil Hrab, "The Green Inquisitor," TCSDaily.com, December 22, 2003.
43. www.ehponline.org/docs/1998/106-4/editorial.html.
44. Mark Hertsgaard, *Vanity Fair*, May 2006.
45. Nick Schulz, "Vanity Scare," , April 14, 2006.
46. Reported at JunkScience.com, August 1, 2006.
47. Ibid.
48. www.oism.org/pproject/.
49. Media Reality Check, "TV's One-Sided Global Warming Nonsense," May 10, 2001.
50. Thomas Sowell, "Global Hot Air," Human Events, February 12, 2007.
51. "The Wal-Mart Posse," *Wall Street Journal*, October 18, 2006.
52. Liza Featherstone, "Down and Out in Discount America," *The Nation*, January 3, 2005.
53. U.S. Department of Labor, www.dol.gov/dol/topic/wages/minimum wage.htm.
54. www.walmartfacts.com/FactSheets/3142007_Corporate_Facts.pdf.
55. www.wakeupwalmart.com/feature/delay/.
56. www.dol.gov/opa/media/press/esa/ESA20050272.htm.
57. "The Wal-Mart Posse," *Wall Street Journal*, October 18, 2006.
58. Ibid.
59. www.walmartmovie.com/about.php.
60. Byron York, "Panic in a Small Town," *National Review*, November 23, 2005.
61. Ibid.
62. Michael Barbaro and Stephanie Strom, "Conservatives Help Wal-Mart, and Vice Versa," *New York Times*, September 8, 2006.
63. John McWhorter, "I Love My Think Tanks," *New York Sun*, September 14, 2006.
64. Corrections, *New York Times*, September 14, 2006.
65. Thomas Sowell, "Cheap Shots," *Washington Times*, September 14, 2006.

66. Kevin A. Hassett, "Unions Wage Vicious, Misguided War on Wal-Mart," Bloomberg News, December 19, 2005.

67. http://article.nationalreview.com/?q=OTdmYjAxOGQzMDJlMzQz
ZTE4MmQ1ZDkxNTY0MDRiM2M=.

68. Ann Pelo and Kendra Pelojoaquin, "Why We Banned Legos," *Rethinking Schools*, Winter 2006.

69. http://amerpundit.com/archives/605.

Chapter 6

1. Jane Smiley, "The Unteachable Ignorance of the Red States," Slate.com, November 4, 2004.

2. Gallup Poll, November 11, 2003.

3. Brad Miner, *Good Order* (New York: Touchstone, 1995).

4. Brad Miner, *The Concise Conservative Encyclopedia* (New York: Free Press, 1996).

5. Ibid.

6. Jean-Jacques Rousseau, *The Social Contract*, trans. Maurice Cranston (New York: Penguin, 1968).

7. Op. cit., Burke, *Reflections on the Revolution in France.*

8. Amy H. Sturgis, "The Rise, Decline, and Reemergence of Classical Liberalism," LockeSmith Institute, 1994, www.belmont.edu/locke smith/liberalism_essay/index.html.

9. Thomas Jefferson, Letter to Samuel Kercheval, July 12, 1810, in *Jefferson: Writings*, (New York: Library of America, 1994).

10. Thomas Jefferson, Letter to John Taylor, May 28, 1816, in *Jefferson: Writings*, (New York: Library of America, 1994).

11. Morris P. Fiorina, "Beyond Reed and Blue," *Stanford Magazine*, September/October, 2006.

12. Sheryl Gay Stolberg, "Bush Assures That the Nation Is Safer as Memories Turn to a Day of Destruction," *New York Times*, September 8, 2006.

13. William Voegeli, "True Smears," The Remedy (the Claremont Institute blog), September 8, 2006.

14. Peter Berkowitz, "Illiberal Liberalism," *First Things*, April 2007.

15. David McCullough, "A Man Worth Knowing, *Imprimis*, May 2006.

16. David Lehman, "From Euphemism to Bloody Lies," *The American Enterprise*, May/June 1999.

17. Op. cit., Smiley.

18. Patrick J. Garrity, "The Long Twilight Struggle," *Wall Street Journal*, September 6, 2006.

19. Dennis McCafferty, "Declaring Our Freedoms," *USA Weekend*, July 2, 2006.

20. www.rippleofhope.net/2002/10/cure-for-war-fever-universal-service .html

21. Ibid.

22. Karl Zinsmeister, "Soldiers of Virtue," *The American Enterprise*, July/ August 1999.

23. William F. Buckley Jr., "On Un-Americanism," *National Review*, October 1, 1990.

24. Ibid.

25. Donna R. LaPlante, "You Can Spit on God, But Don't You Dare Affirm Him," *New Oxford Review*, February 2007.

26. Robert J. Samuelson, "News Cut to Fashion," *Washington Post*, March 13, 1996.

27. Friedrich A. Hayek, *The Road to Serfdom: 50th Anniversary Edition* (University of Chicago, 1994).

28. Quoted in Evan Gahr, "Spirited Enterprise," *The American Enterprise*, July/August 1997.

29. Johan Norberg, "Humanity's Greatest Achievement," *Wall Street Journal*, October 2, 2006.

INDEX